SHOW WHAT YO... ...HE ...OOK

OAT

FOR GRADE 6

MATHEMATICS

grade 6

PREPARATION FOR THE OHIO ACHIEVEMENT TESTS

Show What You Know® Publishing

NAME

Published by:
Show What You Know® Publishing
A Division of Englefield & Associates, Inc.
P.O. Box 341348
Columbus, OH 43234-1348
Phone: 614-764-1211
www.showwhatyouknowpublishing.com
www.passtheoat.com

Information obtained from the Ohio Department of Education web site, April 2007.

Printed in the United States of America
09 08   20 19 18 17 16 15 14 13 12 11 10 9 8 7 6 5 4 3

ISBN: 1-59230-281-5

Acknowledgements

Show What You Know® Publishing acknowledges the following for their efforts in making this assessment material available for Ohio students, parents, and teachers.

Cindi Englefield, President/Publisher
Eloise Boehm-Sasala, Vice President/Managing Editor
Christine Filippetti, Production Editor
Jill Borish, Production Editor
Charles V. Jackson, Mathematics Editor
Melissa Blevins, Assistant Editor
Angela Gorter, Assistant Editor
Jennifer Harney, Editor/Illustrator

About the Contributors

The content of this book was written BY teachers FOR teachers and students and was designed specifically for the Ohio Achievement Test (OAT) for Grade 6 Mathematics. Contributions to the Mathematics chapter of this book were also made by the educational publishing staff at Show What You Know® Publishing. Dr. Jolie S. Brams, a clinical child and family psychologist, is the contributing author of the Test Anxiety and Test-Taking Strategies chapters of this book. Without the contributions of these people, this book would not be possible.

Table of Contents

Introduction

Introduction

The purpose of the Ohio Achievement Test (OAT) is to measure student learning. Throughout the school year, students are exposed to a wide variety of concepts from a range of subjects, only some of which are tested by the Mathematics OAT. Yet it is important that all Ohio Academic Content Standards be taught in order to ensure that students have a well-rounded understanding of the sixth-grade curriculum. Students who have been taught the elements of this curriculum will have been exposed to all that is assessed by the Mathematics OAT. Nonetheless, students will benefit from the review of key details as they prepare to take this assessment.

The *Show What You Know® on the OAT for Grade 6 Mathematics, Student Workbook* is designed to help students better understand the types of information they will see on the Mathematics OAT. This book will help students review important elements assessed by the Mathematics OAT; it is not a substitute for continuous teaching and learning, which take place both in and outside the classroom. But, as with any assessment, it is a good idea to review principles that have been taught and learned prior to taking the Mathematics OAT.

It is impossible to cover everything students have learned throughout their life in one book. However, students can use this book to refresh their memory and to brush up on their test-taking skills. This book is full of practice questions, test-taking hints, and problem-solving strategies—all of which were designed to help students show what they know. *Show What You Know® on the OAT for Grade 6 Mathematics, Student Workbook* includes many features that will benefit students as they prepare for the OAT:

- The first two chapters—Test Anxiety and Test-Taking Strategies—were written especially for sixth students. Test Anxiety offers advice on how to reduce anxious feelings about tests, and Test-Taking Strategies gives strategies students can use to do their best on tests.

- The Mathematics Tutorial chapter of this book contains introductory material about the test, including Item Distribution and Scoring Information. The Mathematics Tutorial contains multiple-choice, short-answer, and extended-response questions. A sample Answer Document page is located next to the question to help students become familiar with how to write their answer in the space allowed. An analysis for each tutorial question is given to help students identify the correct answer.

- The Mathematics Practice Test chapters of this book each contain one 40-question practice test and an Answer Document. The questions are multiple choice, short answer, and extended response.

For easy reference, this Student Workbook correlates with the *Show What You Know® on the OAT for Grade 6 Mathematics, Parent/Teacher Supplement* (sold separately).

Good luck on the OAT!

Test Anxiety

What is Test Anxiety?

Test anxiety is just a fancy name for feeling nervous about tests. Everyone knows what it is like to be nervous. Feeling nervous is not a good experience!

Lots of students have anxiety about taking tests, so if you are a test worrier, don't let it worry you! Most likely, many of your fellow students and friends also have fearful feelings about tests but do not share these feelings with others. Sixth grade is a time when everyone wants to seem "grown up," and few sixth graders want to look weak or afraid in the eyes of their friends or their teachers. But not talking to others about anxiety only makes the situation worse. It makes you feel alone and also makes you wonder if there is something "wrong" with you. Be brave! Talk to your friends and teachers about test anxiety. You will feel better for sharing.

What Does It Feel Like to Have Test Anxiety?

Students who have test anxiety don't always feel the same way, but they always feel bad! Here are some ways that students feel when they are anxious about tests.

- **Students who have test anxiety rarely think good things about themselves.**
  They lack confidence in their abilities, and they are convinced they will do poorly on tests. Not only do they feel bad about themselves and their abilities, but they just can't keep negative thoughts out of their minds. They would probably make terrible detectives, because in spite of all the good things they could find out about themselves, they only think about what they can't do. And that's not the worst of it! Students with test anxiety also exaggerate. When they think of the smallest problem, it becomes a hundred times bigger, especially when they think about tests. They are very unforgiving of themselves. If they make a mistake, they always think the worst or exaggerate the situation. If they do poorly on a quiz, they never say, "Well, it's just a quiz, and I'll try better next time." Instead they think, "That test was terrible and I can only imagine how badly I'll do next week." For students with test anxiety, there is never a brighter day ahead. They don't think many good thoughts about themselves, and they certainly don't have a happy outlook on their lives.

- **Students who have test anxiety have poor "thinking habits."**
  Negative thinking is a habit just like any other habit. Some habits are good and some habits are bad, but negative thinking is probably the worst habit of all. A habit forms when you do something over and over again until it becomes so much a part of you that you don't think about it anymore. Students with test anxiety develop negative ways of thinking about themselves and about schoolwork, especially about tests. They tend to make the worst out of situations and imagine all kinds of possibilities that probably will not happen. Their thoughts grow like a mushroom out of control! Besides having negative ideas about tests, they begin to have negative ideas about most everything else in their lives. This is not a good way of thinking because the more poorly they feel about themselves, the worse they do in school, and bad grades make them feel even worse about themselves. What a mess! Students who have constant negative thoughts about themselves and schoolwork probably have test anxiety.

- **Students who have test anxiety may feel physically uncomfortable or even ill.**
  It is important to know that your mind and body are connected. What goes on in your mind can change how your body feels, and how your body feels can influence what goes on in your thinking. When students have test anxiety, their thoughts might cause them to have physical symptoms which include a fast heartbeat, butterflies in the stomach, headaches, and all sorts of other physical problems. Some kids become so ill they end up going to the doctor because they believe they are truly sick. Some students miss a lot of school due to anxiety, but they aren't really ill. Instead, their thoughts are controlling their bodies in a negative way. Some anxious students do not realize that what they are feeling is anxiety. They miss many days of school, not because they are lazy or neglectful, but because they believe they truly are not feeling well. Unfortunately, the more school they miss, the more behind they are and the more nervous they feel. Students who suffer from test anxiety probably feel even worse on test days. Their uncomfortable physical feelings will make them either avoid the test completely or feel so bad during the test that they do poorly. Guess what happens then. They feel even worse about themselves, become more anxious, and the cycle goes on and on.

- **Students who have test anxiety "freak out" and want to escape.**

  Many students feel so bad when they are anxious that they will do anything to avoid that feeling. For most students, this means running away from problems, especially tests. Some students try to get away from tests by missing school. This does not solve any problems; the more a student is away from school, the harder schoolwork is, and the worse he or she feels. Some students worry about being worried! It may sound silly, but they are worried that they are going to freak out, and guess what happens . . . they do! They are so terrified that they will have uncontrollable anxious feelings that they actually get anxious feelings when thinking about this problem! For many students, anxiety is such a bad feeling that they will do anything not to feel anxious, even if it means failing tests or school. Although they know this will cause them problems in the future, their anxiety is so overwhelming they would rather avoid anxiety now and fail later. Unfortunately, this is usually what happens.

- **Students who have test anxiety do not show what they know on tests.**

  Students who have test anxiety do not make good decisions on tests. Instead of focusing their thoughts, planning out their answers, and using what they know, students find themselves "blanking out." They stare at the paper, and no answer is there! They become "stuck" and cannot move on. Some students come up with the wrong answers because their anxiety gets in the way of reading directions carefully and thinking about answers thoughtfully. Their minds are running in a hundred different ways and none of those ways seem to be getting them anywhere. They forget to use what they know, and they also forget to use study skills that can help them do their best. When students are so worried that they cannot make good decisions and use all of the talents they have, it is called test anxiety.

Are You One of These "Test-Anxious" Sixth Graders?

As you have seen, students with test anxiety have negative thoughts about themselves, often feel anxious to the point of being ill, freak out and want to escape, and rarely show what they know on tests. Do any of the following kids remind you of yourself?

Stay-Away Stephanie

Stephanie's thoughts tell her it is better to stay away from challenges, especially tests. Stephanie is a good girl, but she is always in trouble at school for avoiding tests. Sometimes, she really feels ill and begs her mom to allow her to stay home on test days. At other times, Stephanie does anything to avoid school, refusing to get up in the morning or to leave the house to catch the bus. Stephanie truly believes there is nothing worse than taking a test. She is so overwhelmed with anxiety that she forgets about the problems that will happen when she stays away from her responsibilities. Unfortunately, the more she stays away, the worse the situation becomes. Stay-Away Stephanie feels less nervous when she doesn't face a test, but she never learns to face her fears.

Worried Wendy

Wendy is the type of sixth grader who always expects the worst thing to happen. She has many negative thoughts. Even when situations have turned out to be OK, Wendy focuses on the few bad things that happened. She exaggerates negative events and forgets about everything good. Her mind races a mile a minute with all sorts of thoughts and ideas about tests. The more she thinks, the worse she feels, and her problems become unbelievably huge. Instead of just worrying about a couple of difficult questions on a test, she finds herself thinking about failing the whole test, being made fun of by her friends, being grounded by her parents, and never going to college. She completely forgets that her parents would never be so strict, that her friends like her for many more reasons than her test grades, and that she has all sorts of career choices ahead of her. No one is going to hold it against her if she performs poorly on a test. It is not going to ruin her life. However, Wendy believes all of that would happen. Her negative thoughts get in the way of thinking anything positive.

Critical Chris

Chris is the type of sixth grader who spends all of his time putting himself down. No matter what happens, he always feels he has been a failure. While some people hold grudges against others, Chris holds grudges against himself. No matter what little mistakes he makes, he can never forget them. Chris has had many good things happen to him in his life, and he has been successful many times. Unfortunately, Chris forgets all the good and only remembers the bad. Because he doesn't appreciate himself, Chris has test anxiety.

Victim Vince

Most sixth graders find it is important to take responsibility for their actions. It helps them understand that adulthood is just around the corner, and that they are smarter and more able than they ever thought they were. However, Vince is not like this. He can't take responsibility for himself at all. He thinks everything is someone else's fault and constantly complains about friends, parents, schoolwork, and especially tests. He tells himself, "They make those tests too hard." He sees the teachers as unfair, and he thinks life is generally against him. Vince does not feel there is anything he can do to help his situation, and there is little he thinks he can do to help himself with tests. Because he does not try to learn test-taking skills or to understand why he is afraid, he continues to feel hopeless and angry. Not surprisingly, he does poorly on tests, which only makes his thoughts about the world around him worse.

Perfect Pat

Everyone knows that there is more homework and responsibility in sixth grade than in previous grades. Everyone in the sixth grade needs to try his or her best, but no one should try as much as Pat does. All Pat does is worry. No matter what she does, it's never good enough. She will write book reports over and over and study for tests until she is exhausted. Trying hard is fine, but no matter what Pat does, she feels she has never done enough. Because she never accomplishes what she sets out to do (that would be impossible!), she worries all the time. Her anxiety level gets higher and higher. The more anxious she becomes, the worse she does on tests. This just makes her study and worry more. What a terrible situation!

How Do I Handle Test Anxiety?

Test anxiety is a very powerful feeling that convinces students they are weak and helpless. Feelings of test anxiety can be so powerful it seems there is nothing you can do to stop them. Anxiety seems to take over your mind and body and leaves you feeling like you are going to lose the test anxiety battle for sure.

The good news is that there are many simple things you can do to win the battle over test anxiety! If you can learn these skills in the sixth grade, you are on the road to success in school and for all other challenges in your life.

- **Change the way you think**
  Most of us don't "think about how we think." We just go along thinking our thoughts and never really considering whether they are helpful or not helpful or if they are right or wrong. We rarely realize how much the way we think has to do with how well we get along in life. Our thoughts can influence how we feel about ourselves, how we get along with other people, how well we do in school, and how we perform on tests.

- **The Soda Pop Test**
  Most sixth graders have heard a parent or teacher tell them, "There is more than one side to any story." One student reported that his grandfather used to say, "There's more than one way to paint a fence." Have you ever considered how you think about different situations? Most situations can be looked at in many ways, both good and bad.

  Take a can of soda pop and put it on your desk or dresser at home. Get out a piece of paper and a pen or a pencil. Now, draw a line down the middle of the paper. On one side, put a heading: "All the bad things about this can of soda pop." On the other side put another heading: "All the good things about this can of soda pop." If you think about that can of soda pop, you might come up with the following chart.

All the bad things about this can of soda pop	All the good things about this can of soda pop
Not an attractive color	Easy-to-read lettering
It's getting warm	Nice to have something to drink
Not much in the can	Inexpensive
Has a lot of sugar	Recyclable aluminum cans

Look how easy it is to write down good things or bad things about a silly can of soda pop! That can of soda pop is not really good or bad, it's just a can of soda pop, but we can either look at it in a positive way or we can think about everything negative that comes to our minds. Doesn't the same thing hold true for tests? Tests are not good or bad in themselves. Tests are just a way to challenge us and see what we know. Challenges can be stressful, but they can also be rewarding. Studying for tests can be boring and can take up a lot of free time, but we can also learn a lot and feel great about ourselves when we study. The way you think about tests will help determine how you do in a test-taking situation. Most importantly, how you feel about tests is related to your level of anxiety about test taking. Students who have negative thoughts and feelings about tests become anxious. Students who think positively are less anxious. To reduce test anxiety, try thinking about tests and testing situations using a positive frame of mind.

- **All or Nothing Thinking**
Nothing is ever as simple as it seems! Sometimes we convince ourselves something is going to be awful or wonderful. Rarely does it turn out that way.

Trouble comes along when students think tests are going to be an awful experience. If you dread something happening, it is only going to make things worse. Also, you may be wrong! Nothing is as terrible as it seems. All the negative thoughts you have about the upcoming test cannot possibly be true. Thinking something is awful or terrible and nothing else only leads to trouble and failure. The more negative you feel about something, the worse things turn out.

Very few things are all good or all bad. This is especially true for tests. Recognizing the bad parts of tests can help you be successful. For example, the fact that you need to study for tests, to pay attention while you are taking tests, and to understand there are probably many more fun things to do in school than take tests are all true thoughts. Good thoughts are just as true, including the good feelings one gets from studying and the chance that you might do well. Having "all or nothing" thinking is going to get you nowhere. Successful and happy students know some experiences are better than others, but they try to look at a situation from all sides.

- **Mind Reading**
Some students believe they can read the minds of their parents and teachers. They assume if they do poorly on the Mathematics OAT, everyone will think they are "dumb" or "lazy." The more their minds create all the terrible things that people may say about them, the more anxious they get. This just increases anxiety and definitely does not help students do well on tests.

- **Catastrophizing**

When people catastrophize, they make everything a catastrophe! A catastrophe is a disaster. It is when something terrible happens. When a student catastrophizes, his or her mind goes on and on creating terrible scenes of disasters. If someone put all these ideas into a movie script, the writer might be rich!

The Mathematics OAT is an important part of a sixth-grader's school year. It is a test that helps the student, the teacher, and the school. However, a sixth-grade student is much more than just his or her score on the Mathematics OAT! Each student is an individual who has his or her own great personality, talents, and other successes in school. If what people catastrophized about was really true, the whole world would be a terrible mess! Imagine if your mother cooked a dinner that didn't turn out quite right. This might mean everyone has to go out for fast food, but you wouldn't love your mother any less. It would be catastrophizing if your mother said, "Now that I burned the dinner, none of my kids will love me. They will probably just want to move out as quickly as they can, and my life will be ruined." Catastrophizing about the Mathematics OAT is just as bad. Thinking that this test is going to be the worst experience of your life and that your future will be ruined will not help you feel comfortable when preparing for and taking the test.

- **Making "Should" Statements**

Students make themselves anxious when they think they "should" do everything! They feel they "should" be as smart as everyone else, "should" study more, and "should" not feel anxious about tests. All these thoughts are pretty ridiculous! You can't always be as smart as the next person, and you do not have to study until you drop to do well on tests. Instead of kicking yourself for not being perfect, it is better to think about all the good things you have done in your life. This will help you do better on tests and be happier in your life by reducing your anxiety.

How Do I Replace Worried Thoughts with Positive Ones?

As we have learned, there are all kinds of thoughts that make us anxious, such as feeling we "should" do everything, thinking we can read peoples' minds, catastrophizing, and thinking only bad thoughts about a situation. Learning how to stop these types of thoughts is very important. Understanding your thoughts and doing something about them help control test anxiety.

People who are worried or anxious can become happier when thinking positive thoughts. Even when situations are scary, such as a visit to the dentist, "positive imagery" is helpful. "Positive imagery" means thinking good thoughts to keep from thinking anxious thoughts. Positive and negative thoughts do not go together! If you are thinking something positive, it is almost impossible to think of something negative. Keep this in mind when test anxiety starts to become a bother.

Try these ideas the next time you find yourself becoming anxious.

- **Thoughts of Success**
  Thinking "I can do it" thoughts can chase away thoughts of failure. Imagine times you were successful, such as when you performed well in a dance recital or figured out a complicated brain teaser. These are good things to think about. Telling yourself you have been successful in the past and can be successful in the future will chase away thoughts of anxiety.

- **Relaxing Thoughts**
  Some people find that thinking calming or relaxing thoughts is helpful. Picturing a time in which you felt comfortable and happy can lessen your anxious feelings. Imagine yourself playing a baseball game, running through a park, or eating an ice cream cone; these are all positive thoughts that may get in the way of anxious ones. Some students find that listening to music on the morning of a test is helpful. It probably doesn't matter what music you listen to, as long as it makes you feel good about yourself, confident, and relaxed.

  Just as you can calm your mind, it is also important for you to relax your body. Practice relaxing your body. When students have test anxiety, their muscles become stiff. In fact, the whole body becomes tense. Taking deep breaths before a test and letting them out slowly as well as relaxing muscles in your body are all very helpful ways to feel less anxious. Your school counselors will probably have more ideas about relaxation. You may find that relaxation doesn't just help you on tests, but is helpful for other challenging situations and for feeling healthy overall.

- **Don't Let Yourself Feel Alone**
  Everyone feels more anxious when they feel alone and separate from others. Talking to your friends, parents, and teachers about your feelings helps. Feeling anxious about tests does not mean there is something wrong with you. You will be surprised to find that many of your friends and fellow students also feel anxious about tests. You may be even more surprised to learn your parents and teachers have also had test anxiety. They know what you are going through and are there to support you.

- **Take Care of Yourself**

  Everyone is busy. Many sixth graders are involved in all sorts of activities, including sports, music, and helping around the house. Often, you are so busy you forget to eat breakfast or you don't get enough sleep. Eating and sleeping right are important, especially before a test like the Mathematics OAT. If you are not a big breakfast eater, try to find something that you like to eat and get in the habit of eating breakfast. When you do not eat right, you may feel shaky and have a hard time concentrating, and your anxiety can increase. Being tired does not help either. Try to get in the habit of going to bed at a good time every night (especially the night before a test) so you can feel fresh, rested, and confident for the Mathematics OAT.

- **Practice Your Test-Taking Success**

  People who have accomplished incredibly difficult goals have used their imaginations to help them achieve success. They thought about what they would do step by step to be successful.

  You can do the same! Think about yourself on the morning of the test. Imagine telling yourself positive thoughts and eating a good breakfast. Think about arriving at school and feeling confident that you will do fine on the test. Imagine closing your eyes before the test, breathing deeply, relaxing, and remembering all the study skills you have learned. The more you program your mind to think in a successful and positive way, the better off you will be.

- **Learn to Use Study Skills**

  The next chapter in this book will help you learn test-taking strategies. The more you know about taking tests successfully, the calmer you will feel. Knowledge is power! Practice test-taking strategies to reduce your test anxiety.

- **Congratulate Yourself During the Test**

  Instead of thinking, "I've only done five problems and I've got eight pages to go," or "I knew three answers right, but one mixed me up," reward yourself for what you have done. Tell yourself, "I got some answers right so far, so I bet I can do more." After all, if you don't compliment yourself, who will?

Conclusion

You are not alone if you feel stressed about tests. It is probably good to feel a little anxious, because it motivates you to do well. However, if you feel very anxious about tests, then reading, re-reading, and practicing the suggestions in this chapter will help you tackle your test anxiety.

Test-Taking Strategies

All Students Can Do Their Best on Tests

Most students want to do their best on tests. Tests are one important way for teachers to know how well students are doing and for students to understand how much progress they are making in their studies. Tests like the Mathematics OAT help schools measure how well students are learning so teachers and principals can make their schools even better. Students can do the best job possible in "showing what they know" by learning how to be good test takers.

It's just not possible to do a good job without the right tools. Test-taking strategies are tools to help you perform well on tests. Everyone needs good tools and strategies when facing a problem. If you do not have these, even the smartest or most talented person will do poorly. Think about people who are wizards at fixing cars and trucks. Your family's car dies in the middle of the road. The situation looks pretty hopeless. How are you ever going to get to that basketball game tomorrow if your parent's car is a mechanical mess? Suddenly, magic happens! The mechanic at the repair shop calls your parents and tells them the car is ready, just a day after it broke down. How did this happen? It happened because the auto-repair mechanic had a great deal of knowledge about cars. Most importantly, he had the right tools and strategies to fix the car. He knew how to look at the problem, and when he figured out what to do, he had some special tools to get the job done. You can also find special ways that will help you be a successful test taker.

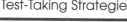
Tools You Can Use on the Mathematics OAT and Tests Throughout Your Life!

Be An "Active Learner."

You can't learn anything by being a "sponge." Just because you are sitting in a pool of learning (your classroom) does not mean you are going to learn anything just by being there. Instead, students learn when they actively think and participate during the school day. Students who are active learners pay attention to what is being said. They also constantly ask themselves and their teachers questions about the subject. When able, they participate by making comments and joining discussions. Active learners enjoy school, learn more, feel good about themselves, and usually do better on tests. Remember the auto-repair mechanic? That person had a lot of knowledge about fixing cars. All the tools and strategies in the world will not help unless you have benefited from what your teachers have tried to share.

Being an active learner takes time and practice. If you are the type of student who is easily bored or frustrated, it is going to take some practice to use your classroom time differently. Ask yourself the following questions.

- Am I looking at the teachers?

- Do I pay attention to what is being said?

- Do I have any questions or ideas about what the teacher is saying?

- Do I listen to what my fellow students are saying and think about their ideas?

- Do I look at the clock and wonder what time school will be over, or do I appreciate what is happening during the school day and how much I can learn?

- Do I try to think about how my schoolwork might be helpful to me now or in the future?

Although you do need special tools and strategies to do well on tests, the more you learn, the better chance you have of doing well on tests. Think about Kristen!

There was a young girl named Kristen,
Who was bored and wouldn't listen.
She didn't train
To use her smart brain
And never knew what she was missing!

Don't Depend on Luck!

Preparing for the Mathematics OAT might feel stressful or boring at times, but it is an important part of learning how to show what you know and doing your best. Even the smartest student needs to spend time taking practice tests and listening to the advice of teachers about how to do well. Luck alone is not going to help you do well on the Mathematics OAT or other tests. People who depend on luck do not take responsibility for themselves. Some people who believe in luck do not want to take the time and effort to do well. It is easier for them to say, "It's not my fault I did poorly. It's just not my lucky day." Some people just do not feel very good about their abilities. They get in the habit of saying, "Whatever happens will happen." They believe they can never do well no matter how much they practice or prepare. Students who feel they have no control over what happens to them usually have poor grades and do not feel very good about themselves.

Your performance on the Mathematics OAT (and other tests) is not going to be controlled by luck. Instead, you can have a lot of control over how well you do in many areas of your life, including test taking. Don't be like Chuck!

There was a cool boy named Chuck,
Who thought taking tests was just luck.
He never prepared.
He said, "I'm not scared."
When his test score appears, he should duck!

Do Your Best Every Day!

Many students find sixth grade much different than other grades. Suddenly, the work seems really hard! Not only that, but your teachers are no longer treating you like a baby. That's good in some ways, because it gives you more freedom and responsibility, but there sure is a lot to learn! You might feel the same way about the Mathematics OAT; you may feel you'll never be prepared. Many times when we are faced with new challenges, it is easy to just give up.

Students are surprised when they find that if they just set small goals for themselves, they can learn an amazing amount! If you learn just one new fact every day of the year, at the end of the year, you will know 365 new facts. You could use those to impress your friends and family! Now think about what would happen if you learned three new facts every day. At the end of the year, you would have learned 1,095 new facts! Soon you will be on your way to having a mind like an encyclopedia.

When you think about the Mathematics OAT or any other academic challenge, try to focus on what you can learn step by step and day by day. You will be surprised how all of this learning adds up to make you one of the smartest sixth graders ever! Think about Ray!

There was a smart boy named Ray,
Who learned something new every day.
He was pretty impressed
With what his mind could possess.
His excellent scores were his pay!

© Englefield & Associates, Inc.

Get to Know the Mathematics OAT!

Most sixth graders are probably pretty used to riding in their parents' cars. They know how to make the air-conditioning cooler or warmer, how to change the radio stations, and how to adjust the volume on the radio. Think about being a passenger in a totally unfamiliar car. You might think, "What are all those buttons? How do I even turn on the air conditioner? How do I make the window go up and down?" Now, think about taking the Mathematics OAT. The Mathematics OAT is a test, but it may be different than some tests you have taken in the past. The more familiar you are with the types of questions on the Mathematics OAT and how to record your answers, the better you will do. Working through the Mathematics Tutorial and Practice Test chapters in this book will help you get to know the Mathematics OAT. Becoming familiar with the Mathematics OAT is a great test-taking tool. Think about Sue!

There was a kid named Sue,
Who thought her test looked new.
"I never saw this before!
How'd I get a bad score?"
If she practiced, she might have a clue!

Read Directions and Questions Carefully!

One of the worst mistakes a student can make on the Mathematics OAT is to ignore directions or to read questions carelessly. By the time some students are in the sixth grade, they think they have heard every direction or question ever invented, and it is easy for them to "tune out" directions. Telling yourself, "These directions are just like other directions," or "I'm not really going to take time to read this question because I know what the question will be," are not good test-taking strategies. It is impossible to do well on the Mathematics OAT without knowing what is being asked.

Reading directions and questions slowly, repeating them to yourself, and asking yourself if what you are reading makes sense are powerful test-taking strategies. Think about Fred!

There was a nice boy named Fred,
Who forgot almost all that he read.
The directions were easy,
But he said, "I don't need these."
He should have read them instead.

Know How to Fill in Those Answer Bubbles!

Most sixth graders have taken tests that ask them to fill in answer bubbles. You might be a very bright sixth grader, but you will never "show what you know" unless you fill in the answer bubbles correctly. Don't forget: a computer will be "reading" your multiple-choice question answers. If you do not fill in the answer bubble darkly or if you use a check mark or dot instead of filling the bubble in completely, your smart thinking will not be counted! Look at the examples given below.

● Correct

Practice filling in the answer bubbles here.

✗ Incorrect

○　○　○　○　○　○

Learning how to fill in answer bubbles takes practice, practice, and more practice! It may not be how you are used to answering multiple-choice questions, but it is the only way to give a right answer on the Mathematics OAT. Think about Kay!

A stubborn girl named Kay
Liked to answer in her own way.
Her marked answer bubbles
Gave her all sorts of troubles.
Her test scores ruined her day!

Copying is Prohibited

© Englefield & Associates, Inc.

Know How to Use the Answer Grid.

For short-answer and extended-response questions, you will be given an empty grid in which to write your answer. The spaces in the grid can be used to draw pictures if necessary. A sample grid is shown below to give you an idea of how to use the grid correctly.

Joe's original garden was 3 feet by 3 feet, with an area of 9 square feet. If he wants to make the area 16 square feet, he needs his garden to be 4 feet by 4 feet.

Speeding Through the Test Doesn't Help!

Most students have more than enough time to read all of the passages and answer all the questions on the Mathematics OAT. There will always be some students who finish the test more quickly than others, but this does not mean the test was easier for them or their answers are correct. Whether you finish at a faster rate or at a slower rate than other students in your class is not important. As long as you take your time, are well prepared, concentrate on the test, and use some of the skills in this book, you should be able to do just fine. You will not get a better score just because you finish the test before everyone else. Speeding through a test item or through the whole Mathematics OAT does not help you do well. In fact, students do their best when they work at a medium rate of speed, not too slow and not too fast. Students who work too slowly tend to get worried about their answers and sometimes change correct answers into incorrect ones. Students who work too fast often make careless mistakes, and many of them do not read directions or questions carefully. Think about Liz.

There was a sixth grader named Liz,
Who sped through her test like a whiz.
She thought she should race
At a very fast pace,
But it caused her to mess up her quiz.

Answer Every Question!

There is no reason that you should not attempt to answer every question you encounter on the Mathematics OAT. Even if you don't know the answer, there are ways for you to increase your chances of choosing the correct response. Use the helpful strategies described below to help you answer every question to the best of your ability.

- **If you don't know the answer, guess!**

  Did you know that on the Mathematics OAT there is no penalty for guessing? That is really good news! That means you have a one out of four chance of getting a multiple-choice question right, even if you just close your eyes and guess! That means that for every four questions you guess, you should get about 25% (1 out of 4) of the questions right. Guessing alone is not going to make you a star on the Mathematics OAT, but leaving multiple-choice items blank is not going to help you either.

  Now comes the exciting part! If you can rule out one of the four answer choices, your chances of answering correctly are now one out of three. You can almost see your Mathematics OAT score improving right before your eyes!

  Although it is always better to be prepared for the test and to study in school, we all have to guess at one time or another. Some of us do not like to guess because we are afraid of choosing the wrong answer, but on the Mathematics OAT, guessing is better than leaving a question unanswered. Think about Jess!

  There was a smart girl named Jess,
  Who thought it was useless to guess.
  If a question was tough,
  She just gave up.
  This only added to her stress.

- **Use a "code" to help you make good guesses on the Mathematics OAT.**

  Some students use a "code" to rate each answer when they feel they might have to guess. Using your pencil in the test booklet, you can mark the following codes next to each multiple-choice response so you can make the best possible guess. The codes are as follows:

  (+) Putting a "plus sign" by your answer means you are not sure if this answer is correct, but you think this answer is probably more correct than the others.

  (?) Putting a "question mark" by your answer means you are unsure if this is the correct answer, but you don't want to rule it out completely.

  (–) Putting a "minus sign" by your answer means you are pretty sure this is the wrong answer. You should then choose from the other answers to make an educated guess.

  Remember, it is fine to write in your test booklet. Think about Dwight!

  There was a smart kid named Dwight,
  Who marked answers that looked to be right.
  He'd put a plus sign
  Or a dash or a line.
  Now the whole world knows he is bright!

- **Use what you know to "power guess."**

  Not everything you know was learned in a classroom. Part of what you know comes from just living your life. When you take the Mathematics OAT, you should use everything you have learned in school, but you should also use your experiences outside the classroom to help you answer questions correctly. Using your "common sense," as well as other information you know, will help you do especially well on the Mathematics OAT. Try to use what you know from the world around you to eliminate obviously wrong answers. If you can rule out just one answer that you are certain is not correct, you are going to greatly increase your chances of guessing another answer correctly. For example, Think about Drew!

  There was a boy named Drew,
  Who forgot to use what he knew.
  He had lots of knowledge.
  He could have been in college!
  But his right answers were few.

- ## Do Not Get Stuck on One Question!
  One of the worst things you can do on the Mathematics OAT is to get stuck on one question. The Mathematics OAT gives you many chances to show all that you have learned. Not knowing the answer to one or two questions is not going to hurt your test results very much.

  When you become stuck on a question, your mind plays tricks on you. You begin to think that you are a total failure, and your worries become greater and greater. This worrying gets in the way of your doing well on the rest of the test. Remember, very few students know all the answers on the Mathematics OAT. If you are not sure of the answer after spending some time on it, mark it in your test booklet and come back to it later. When you do come back to that question later, you might find a new way of thinking. Sometimes, another question or answer later in the test will remind you of a possible answer to the question that had seemed difficult. If not, you can use your guessing strategies to solve the questions you are unsure of after you have answered all the questions you know. Also, when you move on from a troubling question and find you are able to answer other questions correctly, you will feel much better about yourself and you will feel calmer. This will help you have a better chance of succeeding on a question that made you feel "stuck." Think about Von.

There was a sweet girl named Von,
Who got stuck and just couldn't go on.
She'd sit there and stare,
But the answer wasn't there.
Before she knew it, all the time was gone.

- **Always, and This Means Always, Recheck Your Work!**
Everyone makes mistakes. People make the most mistakes when they feel a little worried or rushed. Checking your work is a very important part of doing your best on the Mathematics OAT. You can read a paragraph over again if there is something you do not understand or something that you forgot. If an answer does not seem to make sense, go back and reread the question. Think about Cath and Jen!

A smart young lady named Cath
Always forgot to recheck her math.
When she was done,
She wrote eleven, not one!
When her test score comes, she won't laugh.

There was a quick girl named Jen,
Who read stuff once and never again.
It would have been nice
If she'd reread it twice.
Her test scores would be better then!

- **Pay Attention to Yourself and Not Others.**

  It is easy to look around the room and wonder how friends are doing on the Mathematics OAT. However, it is important to think about how you are using tools and strategies on the Mathematics OAT. Don't become distracted by friends. You are going to waste a lot of time if you try to figure out what your friends are doing. Instead, use that time to "show what you know."

  If it becomes hard for you to pay attention, give yourself a little break. If you feel you are getting a little tense or worried, or if a question seems tough, close your eyes for a second or two. Think positive thoughts about the Mathematics OAT. Try to put negative thoughts out of your mind. You might want to stretch your arms or feet or move around a little to help you focus. Anything you may do to help pay better attention to the test is a great test-taking strategy. Think about Kirk!

There was a boy named Kirk,
Who thought of everything but his work.
He stared into the air
And squirmed in his chair.
When his test scores come, he won't look!

Understanding the OAT for Grade 6 Mathematics

Introduction

In the Mathematics section of the Grade 6 OAT, you will be asked questions to test what you have learned so far in school. These questions are based on the mathematics skills you have been taught in school through sixth grade. The questions you will answer are not meant to confuse or trick you, but are written so you have the best chance to show what you know.

This chapter contains multiple-choice, short-answer, and extended-response questions. It also contains an Item Distribution chart and scoring information, which show you what type of questions you will see on the Grade 6 Mathematics OAT and a Mathematics Glossary. Finally, the chapter provides additional information about the Mathematics OAT as well as directions on how to use the Mathematics Tutorial chapter.

Questions I Will Answer on the OAT

You will answer multiple-choice, short-answer, and extended-response questions on the Mathematics OAT. Multiple-choice items have four answer choices, and only one is correct. Short-answer items will require you to write a word, phrase, or number sentence. Extended-response items will require you to write a few phrases, a complete sentence or two, or to show your work on a numeric answer.

Examples of a multiple-choice item, a short-answer item, and an extended-response item are shown below.

1. Kia has a rug in her room. It is 10 feet long and 4 feet wide.

    What is the area of Kia's rug?

    A. 14 square feet

    B. 14 cubic feet

    C. 40 square feet

    D. 40 cubic feet

2. Sam is shopping in a department store. He sees a shirt on sale for 55% off of the original price. The original price is $35.00. Tax on the shirt is 6%.

    In your **Answer Document**, determine how much Sam will pay for the shirt. Be sure to include the tax. Show or describe all the steps you use to find the cost of the shirt.

    For question 2, respond completely in your **Answer Document**. (2 points)

3. The stage in the auditorium is 20 meters long and 10 meters wide.

    In your **Answer Document**, create and draw a scale model of the stage.

    State the scale you used and label the dimensions of each side of your model. Show or explain how you determined the length of each side of your model.

    For question 3, respond completely in your **Answer Document**. (4 points)

1. ● ⒝ ⒞ ⒟

The correct answer is A. You should fill in circle A completely.

2. Write your response to question 2 in the space below.

> 55% of $35.00 = .55 × 35 = $19.25
>
> $35.00 – $19.25 = $15.75
>
> 6% of $15.75 = .06 × $15.75 ≈ $0.95
>
> $15.75 + $0.95 = $16.70
>
> Sam will pay $15.75 for the shirt after the 55% discount.
>
> Tax on the shirt will be $0.95.
>
> The total amount Sam will pay for the shirt will be $16.70.

Sam will pay $15.75 for the shirt after the 55% discount. Tax on the shirt will be $0.95. The total amount Sam will pay for the shirt will be $16.70.

3. Write your response to question 3 in the space below.

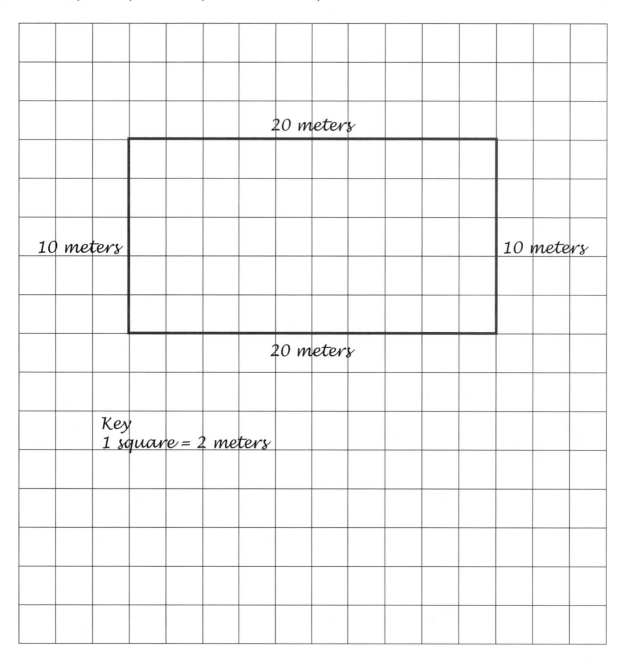

The scale model shown is labeled to show the auditorium stage is 20 meters long and 10 meters wide. The sides are labeled and a key is given showing the scale used as 1 square being equal to 2 meters.

 © Englefield & Associates, Inc.

Item Distribution on the OAT for Grade 6 Mathematics

Standard	Multiple Choice (1 point)	Short Answer (2 points)	Extended Response (4 points)	Points
Number, Number Sense and Operations	7–13	1–3	0–1	13–15
Measurement	4–6	0–2	0–1	8*
Geometry and Spatial Sense	4–7	0–2	0–1	8–9*
Patterns, Functions and Algebra	6–9	0–2	0–1	11–12**
Data Analysis and Probability	4–7	0–2	0–1	8–9**
Number of Scored Items	32	5	2	—
Total Numbers	**39 Items**			**50 points**

* The combined number of points for these two standards on any test form will not exceed 17 points.
** The combined number of points for these two standards on any test form will not exceed 20 points.

Note: This is the Item Distribution that will be used on the actual OAT for Grade 6 Mathematics. Each practice test in this book has 40 questions.

Scoring

Three types of items are used in the Grade 6 OAT Mathematics test: multiple choice, short answer, and extended response. The Mathematics test includes approximately 32 multiple-choice items, five short-answer items (one for each content standard category), and two extended-response items.

Multiple-Choice Items

Multiple-choice items require students to select the correct response from a list of four choices. Each multiple-choice item is worth one point.

Short-Answer and Extended-Response Items

A short-answer item requires students to generate a written response. A short-answer requires a brief response, usually a few sentences or a numeric solution to a straightforward problem. A short-answer item may take up to five minutes to complete, and a student will receive a score of 0, 1, or 2 points per test item.

An extended-response item requires students to generate a written response. An extended-response item requires students to solve a more complex problem or task and to provide a more in-depth response. Students are typically asked to show their work or calculations, explain their reasoning, and justify the procedure used. An extended-response item may require 5 to 15 minutes to complete, and responses receive a score of 0, 1, 2, 3, or 4 points per item. Examples of scoring rubrics can be found on the next page.

Short-Answer Scoring

Short-answer items require a brief written response. Student responses receive a score of 0, 1, or 2 points. Each short-answer item has an item-specific scoring guideline. These written responses may require supporting work or explanations. The following general two-point scoring guideline for short-answer items is used as a template to develop item-specific scoring guidelines for each individual short-answer item.

A **2-point response** provides a complete interpretation and/or correct solution. It demonstrates a thorough understanding of the concept or task. It indicates logical reasoning and conclusions. It is accurate, relevant, and complete.

A **1-point response** provides evidence of a partial interpretation and/or solution process. It demonstrates an incomplete understanding of the concept or task. It contains minor flaws in reasoning. It neglects to address some aspect of the task.

A **Zero-point response** does not meet the criteria required to earn one point. The response indicates inadequate understanding of the task and/or the idea or concept needed to answer the item. It may only repeat information given in the test item. The response may provide an incorrect solution/response and the provided supportive information may be totally irrelevant to the item, or possibly, no other information is shown. The student may have written on a different topic or written "I don't know."

Extended-Response Scoring

Extended-response items require students to demonstrate understanding in depth. Student responses receive a score of 0, 1, 2, 3, or 4 points. Each extended-response item has an item-specific scoring guideline. These written responses may include explanations, appropriate charts, tables, graphs, or other graphic organizers. The following general four-point rubric for extended-response items is used as a template to develop item-specific scoring guidelines for each individual extended-response item.

A **4-point response** provides essential aspects of a complete interpretation and/or a correct solution. The response thoroughly addresses the points relevant to the concept or task. It provides strong evidence that information, reasoning, and conclusions have a definite logical relationship. It is clearly focused and organized, showing relevance to the concept, task and/or solution process.

A **3-point response** provides essential elements of an interpretation and/or a solution. It addresses the points relevant to the concept or task. It provides ample evidence that information, reasoning, and conclusions have a logical relationship. It is focused and organized, showing relevance to the concept, task, or solution process.

A **2-point response** provides a partial interpretation and/or solution. It somewhat addresses the points relevant to the concept or task. It provides some evidence that information, reasoning, and conclusions have a relationship. It is relevant to the concept and/or task, but there are gaps in focus and organization.

A **1-point response** provides an unclear, inaccurate interpretation and/or solution. It fails to address or omits significant aspects of the concept or task. It provides unrelated or unclear evidence that information, reasoning, and conclusions have a relationship. There is little evidence of focus or organization relevant to the concept, task, and /or solution process.

A **Zero-point response** does not meet the criteria required to earn one point. The response indicates inadequate understanding of the task and/or the idea or concept needed to answer the item. It may only repeat information given in the test item. The response may provide an incorrect solution/response and the provided supportive information may be totally irrelevant to the item, or possibly, no other information is shown. The student may have written on a different topic or written "I don't know."

Additional Information

- All work should be done in the Student Workbook. All answers should be written in the Answer Document. By doing so, you will become familiar with answering various types of questions within the spaces provided.
- It is to your benefit to answer all questions.
- You are permitted to use four-function and scientific calculators. These may be provided to you by the school. Test items are designed to be calculator neutral; that is, all items can be completed without using a calculator.

Time Allotment

There is no time limit as you take the Tutorial and Practice Tests in this workbook. You will have two and one-half hours to complete the Mathematics OAT.

Using the Mathematics Tutorial

The Mathematics Tutorial, which begins on page 57, identifies the Content Standards you need to review before taking the actual Mathematics OAT. The Tutorial contains multiple-choice, short-answer, and extended-response questions. A sample Answer Document is located next to the question to help you become familiar with how to write your answer in the space allowed. An analysis for each question is given to help you identify the correct answer.

 © Englefield & Associates, Inc.

Examples of Common Two-Dimensional Shapes

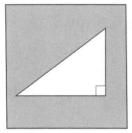

Right Triangle

Isosceles Triangle

Equilateral Triangle

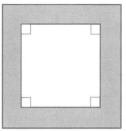

Square

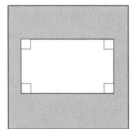

Rectangle

Parallelogram

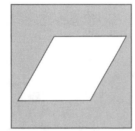

Rhombus

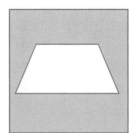

Trapezoid

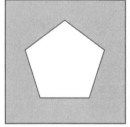

Pentagon

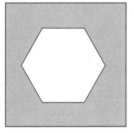

Hexagon

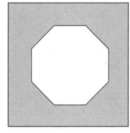

Octagon

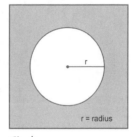

r = radius

Circle

Examples of Common Three-Dimensional Shapes

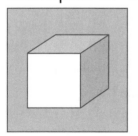

Cube

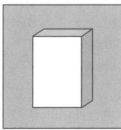

Rectangular Prism

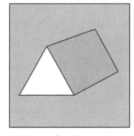

Triangular Prism

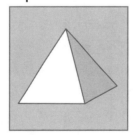

Pyramid

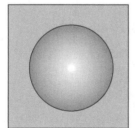

Sphere

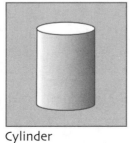

Cylinder

Cone

Examples of How Lines Interact

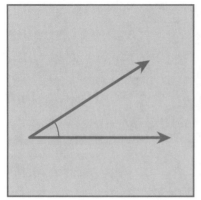

Acute Angle

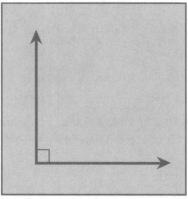

Right Angle

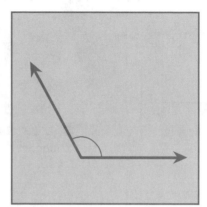

Obtuse Angle

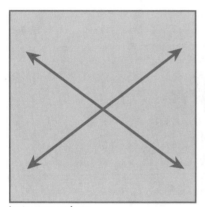

Intersecting

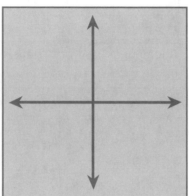

Perpendicular

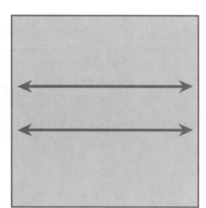

Parallel

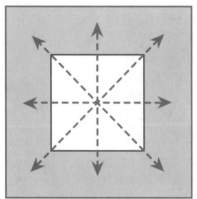

Lines of Symmetry

Examples of Types of Graphs

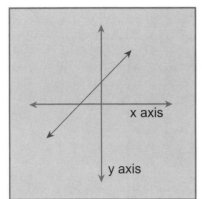

Line Graph

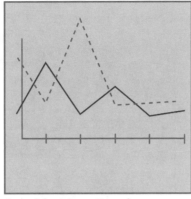

Double Line Graph

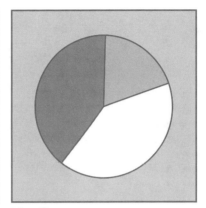

Pie Chart

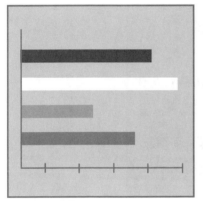

Bar Graph

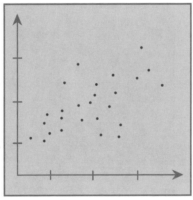

Scatterplot

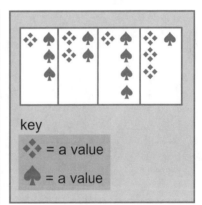

Pictograph

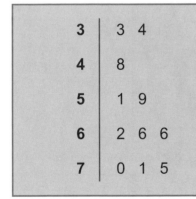

Stem and Leaf Plot

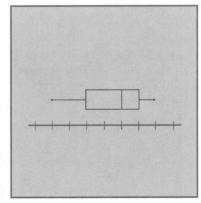

Box and Whisker

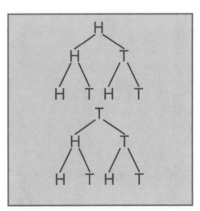

Tree Diagram

Examples of Object Movement

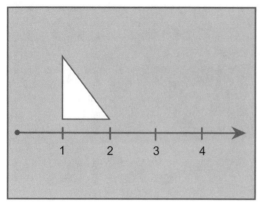 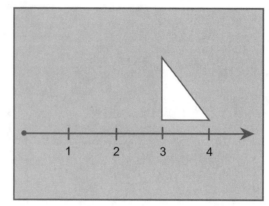

Translation

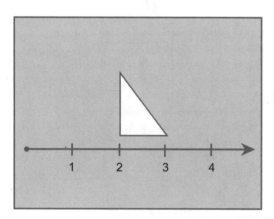 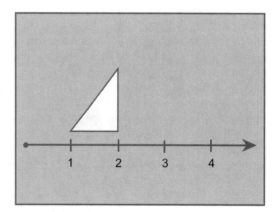

Reflection

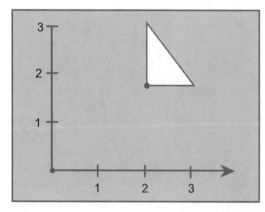 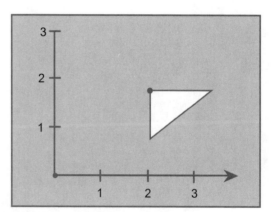

Rotation

Copying is Prohibited © Englefield & Associates, Inc.

Angle Rules

1. All straight lines have 180°.

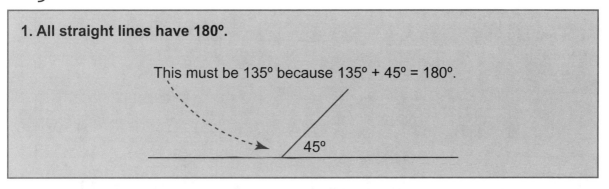

This must be 135° because 135° + 45° = 180°.

45°

2. All triangles have 180°.

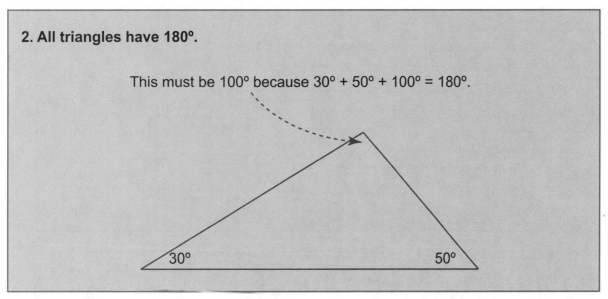

This must be 100° because 30° + 50° + 100° = 180°.

30°

50°

3. Vertical angles are equal (congruent).

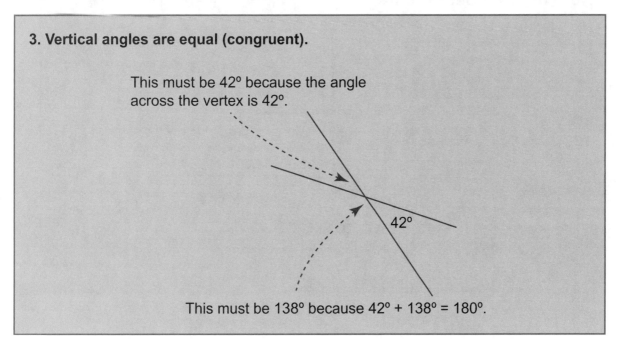

This must be 42° because the angle
across the vertex is 42°.

42°

This must be 138° because 42° + 138° = 180°.

Angle Rules Continued...

4. Alternate interior angles are equal. (Must have parallel lines cut by a transversal.)

This must be 55° because alternate interior angles are equal.

5. If a transversal is perpendicular to one of a pair of parallel lines, then it is also perpendicular to the other.

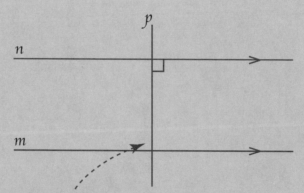

This must be 90° because line m ∥ line n and line n ⊥ line p.

Glossary

absolute value: The non-negative value of any number; the value of any number disregarding its sign; or the distance a number is from zero on a number line; denoted as $|n|$ for any real number n. For example, the absolute value of 4 is 4 and the absolute value of -4 is also 4.

acute angle: An angle that measures less than 90 degrees and greater than 0 degrees.

acute triangle: A triangle with three acute angles.

addend: Any number being added.

addition: An operation joining two or more sets where the result is the whole.

additive identity: The number zero (0). When zero (0) is added to another number the sum is the number itself (e.g., 5 + 0 = 5).

additive inverse property: A number and its additive inverse have a sum of zero (0) (e.g., in the equation 3 + -3 = 0, 3 and -3 are additive inverses of each other).

algebraic equation (or inequality): A mathematical sentence that may contain *variables, constants,* and *operation symbols* in which two *expressions* are connected by an equality (or inequality) symbol. *See also equation and inequality.*

algebraic expression: An expression containing numbers and variables (e.g., 7*x*), and operations that involve numbers and variables (e.g., 2*x* + *y*). Algebraic expressions may or may not contain equality or inequality symbols.

algebraic rule: A mathematical expression that contains variables and describes a pattern or relationship.

altitude: A line drawn from any vertex of a polygon to any side so that the line is perpendicular to the side to which it is drawn. In a three-dimensional figure, it is a line drawn from any vertex of the solid to any face so that the line is perpendicular to the face to which it is drawn. Also known as the height.

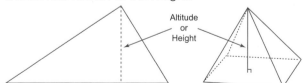

Altitude or Height

analyze: To break down material into component parts so that it may be more easily understood.

angle: The distance, recorded in degrees (°), between two segments, rays, or lines that meet at a common vertex. Angles can be obtuse, acute, right, or straight.

approximate: To obtain a number close to an exact amount.

approximation: The result of obtaining a number close to an exact amount.

area: The amount of two-dimensional space enclosed by a flat object is referred to as its area. The units used to measure area are always some form of square units, such as square inches or square meters. The most common abbreviation for area is A.

argument: A reason or reasons offered for or against something; suggests the use of logic and facts to support or refute a statement or idea.

associative property: This property states that the addition or multiplication of three or more numbers results in the same sum (in addition) or product (in multiplication) regardless of how the numbers are grouped. For example, any numbers a, b, and c, in addition: $(a + b) + c = a + (b + c)$; for multiplication: $(a \times b) \times c = a \times (b \times c)$.

attribute: A characteristic or distinctive feature.

average: A measure of central tendency; generally, the word average usually implies the mean or arithmetic average, but it could also refer to the median or mode. *See mean.*

axes: Plural of axis. Perpendicular lines used as reference lines in a coordinate system or graph; traditionally, the horizontal axis (*x*-axis) represents the independent variable and the vertical axis (*y*-axis) the dependent variable.

bar graph: A graph that uses the lengths of rectangular bars to represent numbers and compare data.

base: Usually refers to the side of a polygon closest to the bottom of the page. In a triangle, the other two sides are called legs. Also, the face around which a three-dimensional object is formed. For example, the base of a triangular prism is a triangle, and the base of a square pyramid is a square.

Glossary

box-and-whisker plot: A type of graph depicted on a number line that is used to express statistical data. The box portion of the graph represents the middle 50% of the given values. The vertical line within the box denotes the median of the data set. The whiskers are extended outward in both directions from the graph and represent the upper and lower 25% of the given values. The extreme points of the whiskers represent the minimum and maximum values of the given data.

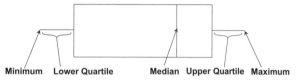

Minimum   Lower Quartile   Median   Upper Quartile   Maximum

break: A zigzag or v-shape on the x- or y-axis in a line or bar graph indicating that the data being displayed do not include all of the values that exist on the number line used. Breaks are very useful when there is a large difference between high and low values in the data set, or when specific values need to be excluded from the scale. For example, weekend days are not needed to chart school attendance, so they can be excluded. There are several different graphic styles of break, but all should be accompanied by a change on one of the graph's scales. Also called an axis break or a squiggle.

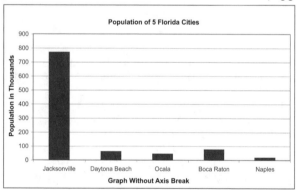

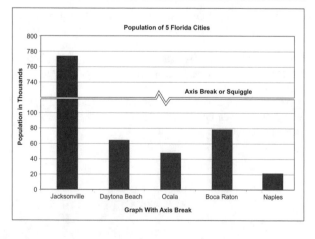

capacity: The amount of space that can be filled in a container. Both capacity and volume are used to measure three-dimensional spaces; however, capacity usually refers to fluid measures, whereas volume is described as cubic units.

central angle: An angle that has its vertex at the center of a circle, with radii as its sides. A central angle and the arc of the circle it subtends have the same measure in degrees.

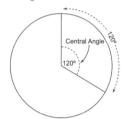

chart: A method of displaying information in the form of a graph or table.

circle: A set of points in a plane that are all the same distance from the center point.
Example: A circle with center point P is shown below.

circle graph: Sometimes called a pie chart; a way of representing data that shows the fractional part or percentage of an overall set as an appropriately-sized wedge of a circle.
Example:

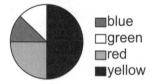

■blue
□green
▨red
■yellow

circumference: The boundary line, or perimeter, of a circle; also, the length of the perimeter of a circle.
Example:

Glossary

closed figure: A two-dimensional figure that divides the plane in which the figure lies into two parts—the part inside the figure and the part outside the figure (e.g., circles, squares, rectangles).

Closed Figures

Open Figures

cluster: In statistics, a relatively large number of data closely grouped around a particular value.

combination: A collection of objects in no particular order. Example: The collection 1, 2, 3 is the same combination as 3, 1, 2.
See permutation.

common denominator: A number divisible by all of the denominators of two or more fractions. Example: The fractions 1/2, 1/3, 1/4 have a common denominator of 12 because 12 is divisible by 2, 3, and 4.

common multiple: A number that is a multiple of each of two or more numbers; used to find a common denominator when operating with fractions having unlike denominators. Example: The number 12 is a common multiple of 2, 3, and 4. *See Multiple.*

commutative property: This property states that the addition or multiplication of two numbers results in the same sum (in addition) or product (in multiplication) regardless of the order of the two numbers. For example, any numbers a and b,
in addition: $a + b = b + a$;
in multiplication: $a \times b = b \times a$.

compare: Look for similarities and differences.

complementary angles: Two angles with a sum of 90°.

composite number: A number that has more than two factors is called a composite number. Examples include 4, 35, and 121. The numbers zero and one are not composite numbers. *See prime number.*

conclude: To make a judgment or decision after investigating or reasoning; to infer.

conclusion: A statement that follows logically from other facts.

cone: A three-dimensional figure with one circular or elliptical base and a curved surface that joins the base to a single point called the vertex.

cones

congruent figures: Figures that have the same shape and size.

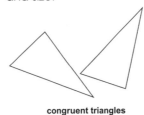

congruent triangles

conjecture: An inference or judgment based on inconclusive or incomplete evidence; a tentative conclusion; a working hypothesis.

constant: A fixed or unchanging quantity. A particular number. The part of a term or expression that is not a variable or operation symbol. Constants are sometimes referred to by special symbols, for example, $\pi \approx 3.1415...$

contraction: A proportional decrease in the size of all dimensions of a figure. Also known as a reduction. A transformation in which a figure grows smaller. Note: Many high school textbooks erroneously use the word dilation to refer to all transformations in which the figure changes size, whether the figure becomes larger or smaller. Unfortunately the English language has no word that refers collectively to both stretching and shrinking. *See dilation.*

contrast: Look for differences.

coordinates: Ordered pairs of numbers that identify the location of points on a coordinate plane. Example: (3, 4) is the coordinate of point A.

counting principle: If a first event has n outcomes and a second event has m outcomes, then the first event followed by the second event has $n \times m$ outcomes.

Glossary

cross-multiply: A method used to solve proportions or evaluate whether or not two fractions are equal. In order to cross-multiply, you must have one fraction on each side of an equals sign to make an equation. Form two products by multiplying each numerator by the denominator of the other fraction: For example, if you are asked whether or not 3/4 equals 6/8, set them equal to one another and cross multiply:

$\frac{3}{4}$ ✕ $\frac{6}{8}$; 3 x 8 = 4 x 6; 24 = 24.

Since these products are equal, the fractions are also equal.

cube: A rectangular prism having six congruent square faces.

customary system: *See U.S. system of measurement.*

cylinder: A solid figure with two circular or elliptical bases that are congruent and parallel to each other connected by a curved lateral surface.

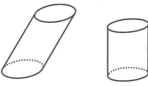

data: Collected pieces of information.

data displays/graphs: Different ways of displaying data in charts, tables, or graphs, including pictographs, circle graphs, single-, double-, or triple-bar and line graphs, histograms, stem-and-leaf plots, box-and-whisker plots, and scatter plots.

decimal number: A number expressed in base 10, such as 39.456 where each digit's value is determined by multiplying it by some power of ten

denominator: The number in a fraction below the bar; indicates the number of equivalent pieces or sets into which something is divided.

dependent variable: A variable whose value is determined by the value of another variable (known as an independent variable.) For example, in the equation $y = x^2$, y is the dependent variable and x is the independent variable. *See independent variable.*

diagonal: A segment joining two non-consecutive vertices of a polygon.

diagram: A drawing that represents a mathematical situation.

diameter: A line segment (or the length of a segment) passing through the center of the circle with end points on the circle.

difference: The number found when subtracting one number from another; the result of a subtraction operation; the amount by which a quantity is more or less than another number.

dilation: A proportional increase in the size of all dimensions of a figure. Also known as an enlargement. A transformation in which a figure grows larger. Note: Many high school textbooks erroneously use the word dilation to refer to all transformations in which the figure changes size, whether the figure becomes larger or smaller. Unfortunately the English language has no word that refers collectively to both stretching and shrinking. *See contraction.*

dimensions: The length, width, or height of an object.

direct measure: Obtaining the measure of an object by using a measuring device, such as a ruler, yardstick, meter stick, tape measure, scale, thermometer, measuring cup, or some other tool. Nonstandard devices such as a paper clip or pencil may also be used.

direct proportion: A method of comparing or solving two equal ratios. For example, if for every 3 people there are 2 dogs, how many dogs will there be for 9 people? The direct proportion to solve this sets the original/known ratio of people to dogs equal to the unknown ratio:

$\frac{3}{2}$ ✕ $\frac{9}{n}$; or $\frac{3}{2}$ ✕ $\frac{9}{6}$.

In this example, the answer derived from the direct proportion is 6. *See cross-multiply.*

distributive property: This property states that the same final answer is found whether a number is multiplied by the sum of two numbers, or whether the first number is multiplied by both of the numbers separately and then the products are added together. For example, for any numbers a, b, and c:
$a \times (b + c) = a \times b + a \times c$.

dividend: A number which is to be divided by another number. Dividend ÷ divisor = quotient.
Example: In 15 ÷ 3 = 5, 15 is the dividend.

$$\text{divisor} \overline{)\text{dividend}}^{\text{quotient}} \qquad 3\overline{)15}^{\,5}$$

Glossary

divisible: One integer is divisible by another non-zero integer if the quotient is an integer with a remainder of zero. Example: 12 is divisible by 3 because 12 ÷ 3 is an integer, namely 4.

division: An operation on two numbers to determine the number of sets or the size of the sets. Problems where the number of sets is unknown may be called measurement or repeated subtraction problems. Problems where the size of sets is unknown may be called fair sharing or partition problems.

divisor: The number by which the dividend is to be divided; also called a factor quotient.
Example: In 15 ÷ 3 = 5, 3 is the divisor.

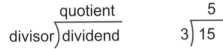

edge: The line segment formed by the intersection of two faces of a three-dimensional figure; a cube has 12 edges.

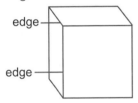

empirical probability: *See experimental probability.*

enlargement: *See dilation.*

equality: Two or more sets of values that are equal.

equally likely: Two outcomes having the same probability of occurring.

equation: A number sentence or algebraic sentence which shows equality between two sets of values. An equation can be recognized by the presence of an equal sign (=).
Examples: 4 + 8 = 6 + 6; 4 + 8 = 24 ÷ 2; 4 + x = 12

equiangular: In any given polygon, if the measures of all of the angles formed by the figure's segments are of equal value (congruent), the polygon is said to be equiangular. All regular polygons are equiangular. Not all polygons that are equiangular are necessarily equilateral. This is illustrated by the diagram below.

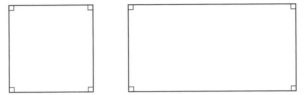

equilateral: Having equal sides. All regular polygons are equilateral. Not all polygons that are equilateral are necessarily equiangular.

equilateral triangle: A triangle with three congruent sides. All equilateral triangles are also equiangular.

equivalent expressions: Expressions that have the same value but are presented in a different format using the properties of numbers.

equivalent forms of a number: The same number expressed in different forms (e.g., $\frac{3}{4}$, 0.75, 75%).

estimate: To find an approximate value or measurement of something without exact calculation.

estimation: The process of finding an approximate value or measurement of something without exact calculation.
• Measurement estimation—an approximate measurement found without taking an exact measurement.
• Quantity estimation—an approximate number of items in a collection.
• Computational estimation—a number that is an approximation of a computation that we cannot (or do not wish to) determine exactly.

evaluate an algebraic expression: Substitute numbers for the variables and follow the algebraic order expression of operations to find the numerical value of the expression.

Glossary

even number: A whole number divisible by two. Examples: 0, 4, and 678 are even numbers.

event: Any subset of the sample space. In rolling a number cube, the event of rolling a "3" is a single event because it contains only one outcome. The event of rolling an "even number" contains three outcomes: 2, 4, and 6.

expanded form: A number written in component parts showing the cumulative place values of each digit in the number.
Example: 546 = 500 + 40 + 6.

experimental probability: Also called empirical probability. The likelihood of an event happening that is based on experience and observation rather than on theory. The ratio of the number of times an event occurs in an experiment to the number of trials.

exponent: When a number is raised to a power, the power it is raised to is expressed by using an exponent. When written, exponents appear after the number they influence and are slightly raised above the number. An exponent can be any rational number, but most commonly, they are whole numbers greater than zero. *See power.* For example:

1. For elementary, middle, and high school: If the exponent is a positive whole number, it shows how many times a number is to be multiplied by itself. (23 = 2 x 2 x 2 = 8 or 46 = 4 x 4 x 4 x 4 x 4 x 4 = 4,096. The "3" and the "6" are the exponents.)

2. For middle and high school: If the exponent is zero, then the value of the expression is one (1) unless the base number is also zero: 20 = 1 or 4970 = 1. The value of zero to the zeroth, 00, is undefined.

3. For high school: If the exponent is a negative whole number, it shows how many times the reciprocal of the number is to be multiplied by itself.

$$2^{-3} = \frac{1}{2^3} = \frac{1}{2} \times \frac{1}{2} \times \frac{1}{2} = \frac{1}{8} \text{ or}$$

$$4^{-6} = \frac{1}{4^6} = \frac{1}{4} \times \frac{1}{4} \times \frac{1}{4} \times \frac{1}{4} \times \frac{1}{4} \times \frac{1}{4} = \frac{1}{4096}$$

4. For high school: If the exponent is a fraction with a numerator of 1, it represents a root of the base.

$$64^{\frac{1}{2}} = \sqrt{64} \text{ or } 64^{\frac{1}{6}} = \sqrt[6]{64}$$

expression: A combination of variables, numbers, and symbols that represent a mathematical relationship.

extraneous information: Information that is not necessary to solving the problem.

extrapolate: To make a guess about a value, function, or graph beyond the values already known. For example, given the sequence of numbers {. . . 2, 4, 6, 8, . . .}, you may predict based on the observed pattern, that the next number in the sequence after 8 is 10 and the number before 2 is 0.

face: A flat surface, or side, of a solid (3-D) figure. This square pyramid has four triangular faces and one square face also called its base.

factor: One of two or more numbers that are multiplied together to obtain a product, or an integer that you can divide evenly into another number. Example: In 4 x 3 = 12, 4 and 3 are factors of 12.

figure: A geometric figure is a set of points and/or lines in 2 or 3 dimensions.

flip: Movement of a figure or object over an imaginary line of symmetry that reverses it, producing a mirror image. Also called a reflection. Examples: Flipping a pancake from one side to the other. Reversing a "b" to a "d". Tipping a "p" to a "b" or a "b" to a "p" as shown below:

fraction: A way of representing part of a whole set. Example:

$$\frac{\text{numerator}}{\text{denominator}} = \frac{\text{dividend}}{\text{divisor}} =$$

$$\frac{\text{\# of parts under consideration}}{\text{\# of parts in a set}}$$

Glossary

function: A relation, such as a graph, in which a variable, called the dependent variable, is dependent on another value, usually an independent variable. In a function, each value of *x* corresponds to only one value of *y*. The graph of a function will pass the "vertical line test."

function machine: Applies a function rule to a set of numbers, which determines a corresponding set of numbers.
Example: Input 9 → Rule x 7 → Output 63. If you apply the function rule "multiply by 7" to the values 5, 7, and 9, the corresponding values are:

$$5 \rightarrow 35$$
$$7 \rightarrow 49$$
$$9 \rightarrow 63$$

function table: A table of *x*- and *y*-values (ordered pairs) that represents the function, pattern, relationship, or sequence between the two variables.

graph: A "picture" showing how certain facts are related to each other or how they compare to one another. Some examples of types of graphs are line graphs, pie charts, bar graphs, scatterplots, and pictographs.

greatest common factor (divisor): The largest factor of two or more numbers; often abbreviated as GCF. The GCF is also called the greatest common divisor.
Example: Find the GCF of 24 and 36:
1) Factors of 24 = {1, 2, 3, 4, 6, 8, 12, 24}.
2) Factors of 36 = {1, 2, 3, 4, 6, 9, 12, 18, 36}.
3) Common factors of 24 and 36 are {1, 2, 3, 4, 6, 12}, the largest being 12.
4) 12 is the GCF of 24 and 36.

grid: A pattern of regularly spaced horizontal and vertical lines on a plane that can be used to locate points and graph equations.

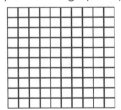

height: *See altitude.*

hexagon: A six-sided polygon. The total measure of the angles within a hexagon is 720°.

regular hexagon   nonregular hexagons

histogram: A graph that shows the frequency distribution for a set of data. A bar represents a range of values and there are no spaces between successive bars.

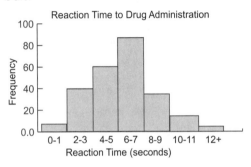

hypotenuse: In a right triangle, the side opposite the right angle. It is always the longest side of a right triangle.

hypothesis: A proposition or supposition developed to provide a basis for further investigation or research.

identity property: This property states that, in addition, the sum of a number and zero always equals the given number. In multiplication, the product of a number and one always equals the given number. For example, for any number *a*, in addition, $a + 0 = 0 + a = a$; in multiplication, $a \times 1 = 1 \times a = a$.

independent variable: A variable whose value determines the value of another variable known as an dependent variable. For example, in the equation $y = x2$, *x* is the independent variable and *y* is the dependent variable.

indirect measure: To obtain data about an object, not by measuring it directly, but by measuring something else or doing some calculation that allows you to infer what the actual measurement must be. Indirect measurement is often used on objects that are very small, very large, or very far away. In other words, indirect measurement is used on objects that are inaccessible for direct measurement.

Glossary

improper fraction: Any fraction in which the numerator has a higher absolute value than the denominator is called an improper fraction. All improper fractions can be converted to mixed numbers. Examples of improper fractions include 9/5, 26/11, 2/1, and 100/10.

independent events: Two events whose outcomes have no effect on one another. Example: The second flip of a coin is independent of the first flip of a coin.

inequality: Two or more sets of values are not equal. There are a number of specific inequality types, including less than (<), greater than (>), and not equal to (≠).

integer: Any number, positive or negative, that is a whole number distance away from zero on a number line, in addition to zero. Specifically, an integer is any number in the set {. . .-3,-2,-1, 0, 1, 2, 3. . .}. Examples of integers include 1, 5, 273, -2, -35, and -1,375.

intercept: A point on a graph where the line crosses the y-axis or x-axis. For a linear equation, an intercept occurs when one of the variables is equal to 0.

interpret: To explain the meaning of information, facts, and/or observations.

intersecting lines: Lines that meet at a point.

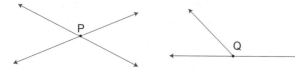

interval: Spacing of (or space between) two numbers on a number line.

inverse property: This property states that, in addition, the sum of a positive number and a negative number with the same absolute value is zero. 4 + (-4) = 0. In multiplication, the product of two reciprocal fractions is one.

$\frac{3}{4} \times \frac{4}{3} = 1$.

For example, for any number a, in addition, $a + \text{-}a = 0$. In multiplication, for any number $b \neq 0$.

$b \times \frac{1}{b} = 1$.

inverse operation: An action that undoes a previously applied action. For example, subtraction is the inverse operation of addition.

irrational numbers: Any real number that cannot be expressed as the ratio of two integers is considered irrational. When written as a decimal, an irrational number neither terminates nor repeats. Some common examples include:

$\sqrt{2}$, $\sqrt{3}$, and π.

isosceles triangle: A triangle with exactly two sides of equal length.

justify: To prove or show to be true or valid using logic and/or evidence.

labels (for a graph): The titles given to a graph, the axes of a graph, or to the scales on the axes of a graph.

least common denominator: The smallest number divisible by all of the denominators of two or more fractions. Example: For 1/12, 3/4, and 2/3, 12 is the least common denominator because 12 is the smallest number that is divisible by 12, 4, and 3.

least common multiple (LCM): The smallest positive multiple of two or more integers.
Example: The number 12 is the LCM of 3, 2, and 4, because it is the smallest number that is a multiple of all three numbers. 12 is also the LCM of 2, -3, 4.

length: A one-dimensional measure that is the measurable property of line segments.

likelihood: The chance that something is likely to happen. *See probability.*

line: One of the so-called undefined terms. As a working definition, think of it as a series of points that extend infinitely in two opposing directions.

line graph: A graph that uses lines, segments, or curves to show that something is increasing, decreasing, or staying the same over time. Note: A line graph does not have to be a straight line

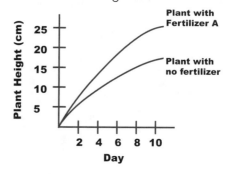

line segment: *See segment.*

Glossary

line of symmetry: A line on which a figure can be folded into two parts that are congruent mirror images of each other, so that every point on each half corresponds exactly to its image on the other half.

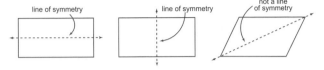

line plot: A line plot, sometimes called a dot plot, starts with a line that represents one variable. The values of the variable are labels on the line. Each observation is marked as a point above the line.

Line Plot for Quality Ratings for
Natural Peanut Butter

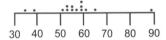

linear equation: An algebraic equation in which the variable quantity or quantities are raised to the zero or first power and the graph is a straight line (e.g., 20 = 2(w + 4) + 2w and y = 3x + 4).

linear inequality: An algebraic inequality in which the variable quantity or quantities are raised to the zero or first power and the graph is a region whose boundary is the straight line formed by the inequality.

mass: The amount of matter in an object.

mean: Also called arithmetic average. A measure of central tendency found by adding the members of a set of data and dividing the sum by the number of members of the set.
Example: If A = 20 children, B = 29 children, and C = 26 children, the mean number of children is found by adding the three numbers (20 + 29 + 26 = 75) and then dividing the sum, 75, by the number 3. So, 25 is the mean of 20, 29, 26. The mean does not have to be a member of the set.

median: The number in the middle of a set of data arranged in order from least to greatest or from greatest to least; or the average of the two middle terms if there is an even number of terms. Example: For the data 6, 14, 23, 46, 69, 72, 94: the median is 46 (the middle number). For the data 6, 14, 23, 69, 72, 94: the median is also 46 (the average of the two middle numbers in the list). The median does not have to be a member of the set.

method: A systematic way of accomplishing a task.

metric system: A measurement system based on the powers of ten. The following is a list of the base units of the metric system, as well as a few of their more common derivatives and abbreviations: length: millimeter, centimeter, meter, kilometer (mm, cm, m, km); volume: cubic centimeter, milliliter, liter (cc, ml, l); weight: grams, kilograms (g, kg); temperature: degrees Celsius (°C); *see U.S. system of measurement.*

midpoint: A point on a line segment that divides the segment into two congruent parts.

mixed number: A number expressed as the sum of an integer and a proper fraction; having a whole part and a fractional part.

Example: $6\frac{2}{3}$

mode: The item that occurs most frequently in a set of data. There may be one, more than one, or no mode. Example: The mode in {1, 3, 4, 5, 5, 7, 9} is 5. If there is a mode, it must be a member of the set.

multiple: A multiple of a number is the product of that number and an integer.
Examples: Multiples of 2 = {2, 4, 6, 8, 10, 12,....}. Multiples of 3 = {3, 6, 9, 12,....}. Multiples of 4 = {4, 8, 12,....}.

multiplication: An operation on two numbers that tells how many in all. The first number is the number of sets and the second number tells how many in each set. Problem formats can be expressed as repeated addition, an array, or a Cartesian product.

multiplicative identity: The number one (1). The product of a number and the multiplicative identity is the number itself (e.g., 5 x 1 = 5).

multiplicative inverse (reciprocal): Any two numbers with a product of 1 (e.g., 4 and $\frac{1}{4}$). Zero (0) has no multiplicative inverse.

mutually exclusive: Two events are mutually exclusive if it is not possible for both of them to occur together. Example: If a die is rolled, the event "getting a 1" and the event "getting a 2" are mutually exclusive since it is not possible for the die to land with both a "1" and a "2" face up on the same roll.

natural numbers: The set of positive integers used for counting, {1, 2, 3, 4, 5, . . .}.

Glossary

negative exponent: Used to designate the *reciprocal* of a number to the *absolute value* of the *exponent*. Also used in scientific notation to designate a number smaller than one (1). For example, 3.45×10^{-2} equals 0.0345.

nonstandard units of measure: Objects such as blocks, paper clips, crayons, or pencils that can be used to obtain a measure.

number line: A line that shows numbers ordered by magnitude from left to right or bottom to top; equal intervals are marked and usually labeled.

number sentence: An expression of a relationship between quantities as an equation or an inequality. Examples: 7 + 7 = 8 + 6; 14 < 92; 56 + 4 > 59.

numerator: The number above the fraction bar in a fraction; indicates the number of equivalent parts being considered.

obtuse angle: An angle with a measure greater than 90 degrees and less than 180 degrees.

obtuse triangle: A triangle with one obtuse angle.

octagon: An eight-sided polygon. The total measure of the angles within an octagon is 1080°.

regular octagon   nonregular octagons

odd number: A whole number that is not divisible by two. Examples: The numbers 53 and 701 are odd numbers.

odds: The ratio of one event occurring (favorable outcome) to it not occurring (unfavorable outcome) if all outcomes are equally likely.

open figure: A two-dimensional figure that is not closed. *See closed figure.*

operation: A mathematical process that combines numbers; basic operations of arithmetic include addition, subtraction, multiplication, and division.

operation symbol: A special symbol that indicates a mathematical operation. Some operation symbols include: +, -, x, ÷, $\sqrt{}$, as well as many others.

operational shortcut: A method having fewer arithmetic calculations.

order of operations: In simplifying an expression involving a number of indicated operations, perform the operations in the following order:
1. Complete all operations inside parentheses first; If there are sets of parentheses inside other sets of parentheses, complete the operations inside the inner-most set first.
2. Calculate powers and roots in the order they occur from left to right;
3. Calculate all multiplications and divisions from left to right;
4. Calculate all additions and subtractions from left to right.

Examples: 7 + 3 x 8 = 31 (multiply 3 x 8 before adding 7); (7 + 3) x 8 = 80 (add 7 and 3 before multiplying by 8); $7 + 3^2 \times 8 = 79$ (square 3, multiply by 8, and then add 7). Sometimes noted with the acronymn PEMDAS.

ordered pairs: Two numbers (elements) for which order is important. When used to locate points on a coordinate graph, the first element indicates distance along the *x*-axis (horizontal), and the second indicates distance along the *y*-axis (vertical).

organized data: Data arranged in a display that is meaningful and that assists in the interpretation of the data. See data displays.

origin: Zero on a number line or the point (0, 0) on a coordinate plane.

outcome: One of the possible results in a probability situation or activity.

outlier: A number in a set of data that is much larger or much smaller than most of the other numbers in the set.

parallel: Two lines, segments, or rays in the same plane that never intersect no matter how far they are extended. The symbol denoting parallel lines is | |.

parallelogram: A quadrilateral with opposite sides parallel.

pattern: An arrangement of numbers, pictures, etc., in an organized and predictable way. Examples: 3, 6, 9 12 or ® 0 ® 0 ® 0.

Glossary

pentagon: A five-sided polygon. The total measure of the angles within a pentagon is 540°.

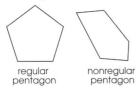

regular
pentagon

nonregular
pentagon

percent: A ratio of a number to 100. Percent means per hundred and is represented by the symbol %.
Example: "35 to 100" means 35%.

perimeter: The total length of the outside border of an object is called its perimeter. For any polygon, the actual value is determined by finding the sum of the lengths of all of its sides. For example, a triangle with sides of 5 inches, 4 inches, and 3 inches has a perimeter of 12 inches. The units of measurement used to express perimeter are linear units, such as inches or kilometers. The most common abbreviation for perimeter is P.

permutation: A collection of objects in a particular order. For example, the word "dormitory" is a collection of nine letters. The same nine letters can spell "dirty room." These arrangements are two different permutations. *See combination.*

perpendicular lines: Lines that lie on the same plane and intersect to form right angles (90 degrees).

90°

pi: An irrational number that expresses the ratio of the circumference of a circle to its diameter. It is represented by the symbol π and is used in circles to find both area and circumference. The exact value of pi cannot be expressed in our number system, but is approximately equal to 3.14 or 22/7.

pictograph: A graph that uses pictures or symbols to represent similar data. The value of each picture is interpreted by a "key" or "legend."

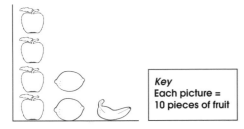

Key
Each picture =
10 pieces of fruit

pie chart: *See circle graph.*

place value: The value of a digit as determined by its place in a number.
Example: In the number 135, the 3 means 3 x 10 or 30. In the number 356, the 3 means 3 x 100 or 300.

plane: One of the so-called undefined terms. As a working definition, think of it as any region that can be defined by a minimum of three noncollinear points and that extends infinitely in a two-dimensional manner. It's like an infinite piece of paper with no thickness.

plane figure: Any arrangement of points, lines, or curves within a single plane, a "flat" figure.

plot: To place points at their proper coordinates on a graph.

point: One of the so-called undefined terms. As a working definition, think of it as a location on a graph defined by its position in relation to the x-axis and y-axis. Points are sometimes called ordered pairs and are written in this form: (x-coordinate, y-coordinate).

polygon: A closed plane figure having three or more straight sides that meet only at their endpoints. Special polygons that have equal sides and equal angles are call regular polygons.

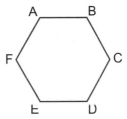

ABCDEF is a polygon.

polyhedron: A solid (3-D) figure having faces that are polygons.

population: A group of people, objects, or events that fit a particular description.

power: When a number is raised by an exponent, it is said to be raised by that power. For example, 3^4 can be thought of as the fourth power of three. To find the actual value, multiply the base number, in this case 3, by itself the number of times equal to the value of the exponent, in this case 4, which equates to 3 x 3 x 3 x 3. Therefore, the fourth power of three equals 81. *See exponent.*

Glossary

precision: An indication of how finely a calculation or measurement is made. In a calculation, it is related to the smallest accurate place values in the numbers. In measurement, it is related to the unit of measurement and the calibration of the tool. Example: Was the measurement made using a ruler marked in increments of 1/4 of an inch or, with more precision, in increments of 1/16 of an inch?

predict: To tell about or make known in advance, especially on the basis of special knowledge or inference.

prediction: A prediction is a description of what will happen before it happens. It is a foretelling that is based on a scientific law or mathematical model.

prime numbers: A whole number greater than 1 having exactly two whole number factors, itself and 1. Examples: The number 7 is prime since its only whole number factors are 1 and 7. One is not a prime number.

prism: A three-dimensional figure that has two congruent and parallel faces (bases) that are polygons; the remaining (lateral) faces are parallelograms. The volume of any right prism is found by multiplying the area of its base, *B*, by its height, h. (*V = Bh*)

probability: The numerical measure of the chance that a particular event will occur, depending on the possible events. The probability of an event, P(E), is always between 0 and 1, with 0 meaning that there is no chance of occurrence and 1 meaning a certainty of occurrence.

product: The result of a multiplication expression; factor x factor = product.
Example: In 3 x 4 = 12, 12 is the product.

proper fraction: Any fraction with the numerator less than the denominator is called a proper fraction. By definition, the value of all proper fractions is less than one. Examples of proper fractions include 1/2, 5/16, 786/5563, and 22/144.

properties: Known interactions of numbers in specific situations. *See associative property, commutative property, distributive property, identity property, inverse property,* and *zero property.*

proportion: *See direct proportion.*

proportional: Constituting a proportion; have the same, or a constant, ratio.

pyramid: A solid (3-D) figure whose base is a polygon and whose other faces are triangles that meet at a common point called the vertex, which is away from the base.

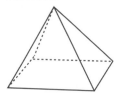

Pythagorean theorem: In any right triangle, the sum of the squares of the lengths of the two sides perpendicular to one another is equal to the square of the length of the hypotenuse: $a^2 + b^2 = c^2$.

quadrant: Any one of four unique sections of a two-dimensional graph. Quadrant I contains the points for which *x* and *y* are both positive; Quadrant II contains the points for which *x* is negative and *y* is positive; Quadrant III contains the points for which *x* and *y* are both negative; and Quadrant IV contains the points for which *x* is positive and *y* is negative.

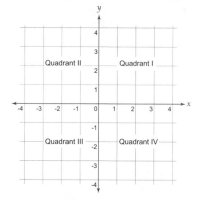

quadrilateral: A four-sided polygon. Some types of quadrilaterals have special names and properties, including rectangles, squares, parallelograms, rhombi, and trapezoids. The total measure of the angles within a quadrilateral is 360°.
Example: ABCD is a quadrilateral.

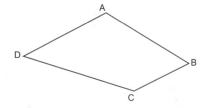

questionnaire: A set of questions for a survey.

Glossary

quotient: The result of dividing one number by another number. Dividend ÷ divisor = quotient. Example: In 15 ÷ 3 = 5, 5 is the quotient.

radical: A mathematical operation symbolized by $\sqrt{}$. A radical is any number or expression that has a root. *See square root.*

radicand: The number that appears within a radical sign (e.g., $\sqrt{25}$, 25 is the radicand).

radius: The distance from the center to the edge of a circle; or, the distance from the center of a circle to a point on the circle.

randomly (chosen): An equal chance of being chosen.

range: In a set of numbers, the difference between the two extremes in the set; in other words, the maximum value in a set minus the minimum value in a set. For example, the range of the set {2, 5, 8, 23, 46} is 46 − 2 = 44.

rate: A rate is an expression of how long it takes to do something. Examples of rates are miles per hour and revolutions per minute. In general, rate is measured as the number of times an event occurs divided by a unit of time.

ratio: A comparison of two numbers using a variety of written forms. Example: The ratio of two and five may be written "2 to 5" or 2:5 or 2/5.

rational number: A number that can be expressed as the ratio of two integers. When written as a decimal, a rational number either terminates or repeats in a recognizable pattern. Examples include 2 (written as a ratio: 2/1), .5 (written as a ratio: 1/2), and 1.75 (written as a ratio: 7/4).

ray: One of the so-called undefined terms. As a working definition, think of it as a half-line. A straight line extending infinitely in one direction from a given point.

real number: Any number that is either rational or irrational is in the set of real numbers. Real numbers are any values you might come across in real life. Examples of real numbers include -2, 0, 0.15, 1/2, $\sqrt{3}$, π, and 7.89×10^9.

reasonable: Within likely bounds; sensible.

reciprocal: When you take any value and raise it to the power of -1, you get its reciprocal. An easy way to think of it is to take the value and make it the denominator of a fraction with a numerator of 1. For example, the reciprocal of 3 is 1/3. Conversely, the reciprocal of 1/3 is 3.

rectangle: A quadrilateral with four right angles. A square is one example of a rectangle.

reduce: To put a fraction into its simplest form by dividing out any common factors. For example, 4/8 reduces to 1/2 in its simplest form.

reduction: *See contraction.*

reflection: A transformation of a figure created by flipping the figure over a line, creating a mirror image. *See flip.*

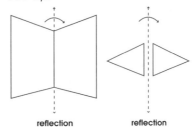

reflection   reflection

regular polygon: A special type of polygon that is both equilateral and equiangular.

relation: A set of ordered pairs (*x, y*).

relative size: The size of one number in comparison to the size of another number or numbers.

represent: To present clearly; describe; show.

rhombus: A quadrilateral with all four sides equal in length. A square is a special type of rhombus

right angle: An angle whose measure is 90 degrees. The lines or segments which form right angles are said to be perpendicular to one another. *See angle.*

Glossary

right circular cylinder: A cylinder in which the bases are parallel circles perpendicular to the side or lateral surface of the cylinder.

right prism or rectangular solid: A three-dimensional figure (polyhedron) with congruent, polygonal or rectangular bases, and lateral faces that are all rectangles.

right triangle: A triangle having one right angle. *See angle and triangle.*

rise: The vertical change on the graph between two points.

rotation: Moving an object around an imaginary point in a circular motion either clockwise or counterclockwise. After the move, the object will have the same shape and size but may be facing a different direction. *See turn.*

rounding: Taking an exact value and making it an approximation. Rounding is done by examining the value of the number in the place value to the right of the place value to which you want to round. If this number is less than 5, you round down; if it is equal to 5 or greater, you round up.

rule: A procedure; a prescribed method; a way of describing the relationship between two sets of numbers. Example: In the following data, the rule is to add 3:

Input	Output
3	6
5	8
9	12

ruler: A straight-edged instrument used for measuring the lengths of objects. A ruler usually measures smaller units of length, such as inches or centimeters.

run: The horizontal change on a graph between two points.

sample: A portion of a population or set used in statistics. Example: All boys under the age of ten constitute a sample of the population of all male children.

sample space: A set of all possible outcomes of a specified experiment.

scale: Sequenced collinear marks, usually at regular intervals or else representing equal steps, that are used as a reference in making measurements.

scale factor: The constant that is multiplied by the length of each side of a figure that produces an image that is the same shape, but not necessarily the same size, as the original figure.

scale model: A model or drawing based on a ratio of the dimensions for the model and the actual object it represents.

scalene triangle: A triangle having no congruent sides.

scatterplot: A type of graph containing points in which coordinates represent paired values. This type of graph is usually used when data seems more random than ordered.

scientific notation: A method of writing any rational number as a decimal number multiplied by some power of ten. It is most often used to represent very large or very small numbers. example: $138{,}000{,}000{,}000 = 1.38 \times 10^{11}$.

segment: One of the so-called undefined terms. As a working definition, think of it as a part of a line ending at specific points. Segments meet at vertices to form closed figures, that are both two- and three-dimensional.

semicircle: Half of a circle with the diameter as its base.

sequence: A set of numbers arranged in a special order or pattern.

set: Any grouping of numbers. A set can be specific or random, small or large. Sets are usually notated by placing numbers within brackets, as with {1, 2, 3}. Before finding statistical data of sets, you should always arrange the values in descending or ascending order.

side: A line segment connected to other segments to form the boundary of a polygon.

←side

Copying is Prohibited

Glossary

similar: Similar polygons must have the same shape, but not necessarily the same size.

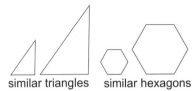

similar triangles   similar hexagons

In order for two polygons to be similar, they must meet two conditions: 1. all pairs of corresponding angles must be congruent, and 2. all pairs of corresponding sides must be proportional. This means that the ratio of the lengths of a pair of corresponding sides must be the same for all other pairs of corresponding sides.

simplify: To take a given mathematical expression and put it into its most basic form, while keeping it equal to its original value. To simplify 4/2, for example, you would change it to 2, because they are equal to one another. To simplify the equation $3n + 2n + 2 + 1$, you would combine the like terms and get $5n + 3$. Simplifying does not necessarily require a specific value to be obtained and should not be confused with solving. *See solve.*

slide: Moving an object a certain distance while maintaining the size and orientation (direction) of the object. This is also known as a translation.
Example: Scooting a book on a table. *See translation.*

slope: The amount of change in the *y*-coordinate with respect to the amount of change in the *x*-coordinate in a straight line on a graph. It is represented by the constant m in the equation $y = mx + b$. Slope can be found by taking any two points on a line, finding the difference in the *y* values, and then dividing that difference by the difference in the corresponding *x* values. The rise over the run.

solid figures: Three-dimensional figures that completely enclose a portion of space (e.g., a prism, cube, sphere, cylinder, cone, and pyramid).
solve: To find the solution to an equation or problem; finding the values of unknown variables that will make a true mathematical statement.

sphere: A closed surface consisting of all points in space that are the same distance from a given point (the center).
Example: A basketball.

square: A rectangle with congruent sides. *See rectangle.*

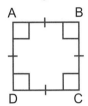

square number: An integer that is a perfect square of another integer. Example: The number 49 is a square number because 49 is the perfect square of 7. (i.e. 49 = 7 x 7).

square root: The square root of a number *A* is the number which when multiplied by itself equals *A*. Example: 7 and -7 are square roots of 49 because 7 x 7 = 49 and (-7) x (-7) = 49. Every positive number has two square roots, one that is positive and one that is negative. The principal square root of a number (denoted $\sqrt{x}$) is its positive square root. Note the difference in the answers to these questions.

1. What is the square root of 81?
   Answer: 9 and -9.

2. What is $\sqrt{81}$?
   Answer: 9 only, not -9.

squiggle: *See break.*

Glossary

standard units of measure: Units of measure commonly used; generally classified in the U.S. as the customary system or the metric system:

Customary System:
  Length
  1 foot (ft) = 12 inches (in)
  1 yard (yd) = 3 feet, or 36 inches
  1 mile (mi) = 1,760 yards, or 5,280 feet

  Weight
  16 ounces (oz) = 1 pound (lb)
  2,000 pounds = 1 ton (t)

  Capacity
  1 pint (pt) = 2 cups (c)
  1 quart (qt) = 2 pints
  1 gallon (gal) = 4 quarts

Metric System:
  Length
  1 centimeter (cm) = 10 millimeters (mm)
  1 decimeter (dm) = 10 centimeters
  1 meter (m) = 100 centimeters
  1 kilometer (km) = 1,000 meters

  Weight
  1,000 milligrams (mg) = 1 gram (g)
  1,000 grams (g) = 1 kilogram (kg)
  1,000 kilograms (kg) = 1 tonne (1 metric ton)

  Capacity
  1 liter (l) = 1,000 milliliters (ml)

---

stem-and-leaf plot: A type of graph that depicts data by occurrence, using commonalities in place value. The digit in the tens place is used as the stem. The digit in the ones place is used as the leaf. Data is arranged like the example below.

Example: Ages of Adults in the Park

Data set				Stem	Leaves
23	25	29	29	2	3 5 9 9
36	38	39	39	3	6 8 9 9
52	54	55	55	5	2 4 5 5

straight angle: An angle with a measure of 180°; this is also a straight line.

strategy: A plan used in problem solving, such as looking for a pattern, drawing a diagram, working backward, etc.

subtraction: An operation that removes sets from an initial set, or finds the difference between two amounts when comparing two quantities.

successive events: Events that follow one another in a compound probability setting.

sum: The result of addition; addend + addend = sum.

summary: A series of statements containing evidence, facts, and/or procedures that support a result.

supplementary angle: Two angles with a sum of 180°.

surface area: The sum of the areas of all of the faces (or surfaces) of a 3-D object. Also the area of a net of a 3-D object. Calculations of surface area are in square units (in^2, m^2, or cm^2).

survey: To get an overview by gathering data.

symbol: A letter or sign used to represent a number, function, variable, operation, quantity, or relationship. Examples: a, =, +, …

symbolic representations of numbers: Expressions represented by symbols (e.g., circles shaded to represent $\frac{1}{4}$ or variables used to represent quantities).

symmetrical: Having a line, plane, or point of symmetry such that for each point on the figure, there is a corresponding point that is the transformation of that point. *See line of symmetry.*

table: A method of displaying data in rows and columns.

tessellation: A pattern formed by placing congruent figures together with no empty space or overlapping areas. An example of a tessellation is a checkerboard.

theoretical/expected probability: The likelihood of an event happening based on mathematical theory rather than on experience and observation.

three-dimensional figure: A shape (geometric figure) having length, width, and height.

transformation: An operation on a geometric figure by which another image is created. Common transformations include reflections (flips), translations (slides), rotations (turns), dilations, and contractions.

Glossary

translation: A transformation of a figure by sliding without turning or flipping in any direction. *See slide.*

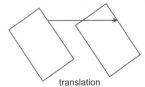
translation

transversal: A line that intersects two or more lines at different points.

trapezoid: Usually a trapezoid is defined as a quadrilateral that has exactly two parallel sides. Less often, it is defined as a quadrilateral with at least two parallel sides. (There is not complete agreement on the definition of a trapezoid.)

tree diagram: A visual diagram of all the possible outcomes for a certain event. A tree diagram is used to show the probability of a certain event happening.

trend: The general direction or tendency of a set of data.

triangle: The figure formed by joining three non-collinear points with straight segments. Some special types of triangles include equilateral, isosceles, and right triangles.The sum of the angles of a triangle is always equal to 180°.

turn: To move a point or figure in a circular path around a center point. Motion may be either clockwise or counterclockwise. Example: The hands of a clock turn around the center of the clock in a clockwise direction. *See rotation.*

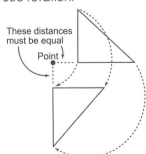
These distances must be equal
Point

two-dimensional figure: A shape (geometric figure) having length and width. (A flat figure)

U.S. system of measurement: This is the system of measurement that most people in the United States use; the rest of the world, for the most part, uses the metric system. The following is a list of common U.S. units of measurement along with their abbreviations: length: inches, feet, yards, miles (in, ft, yd, mi); volume: fluid ounces, teaspoons, tablespoons, cups, pints, quarts, gallons (fl oz, tsp, tbsp, c, pt, qt, gal); weight: ounces, pounds, tons (oz, lb, t); temperature: degrees Fahrenheit (°F). Also called the customary system of measurement.

undefined terms: A term whose meaning is not defined in terms of other mathematical words, but instead is accepted with an intuitive understanding of what the term represents. The words "point," "line," and "plane" are undefined terms from geometry.

unknown: In algebra, the quantity represented by a variable.

unorganized data: Data that are presented in a random manner.

validate: To determine whether a given statement is true. To verify or confirm.

variable: A symbol used to represent a quantity that is unknown, that changes, or that can have different values. Example: In 5*n*, the n is a variable.

verify: To establish as true by presentation of evidence.

vertex: In a two-dimensional object, any point where two segments join to form an angle. In a three-dimensional object, any point where three or more segments join to form a corner of the object. In a cube, for example, there are 8 vertices.

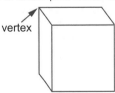
vertex

vertical angles: The pair of angles opposite to one another at the point where two lines, segments, or rays intersect. Vertical angles are always congruent to one another.

vertices: Plural of vertex.

Glossary

volume: The amount of area taken up by a three-dimensional object is known as its volume. The units of measurement used to express volume can be cubic units, such as cubic feet or cubic centimeters, or, when measuring fluids, units such as gallons or liters. Volume is usually abbreviated as V and is also called capacity.

whole number: An integer in the set {0, 1, 2, 3 . . .}. In other words, a whole number is any number used when counting, in addition to zero.

weight: Measures that represent the force of gravity on an object.

word forms: The expression of numbers and/or symbols in words. Examples: 546 is "five hundred forty-six." The "<" symbol means "is less than." The ">" symbol means "is greater than." The "=" symbol means "equals" or "is equal to."

x-axis: One of two intersecting straight (number) lines that determine a coordinate system in a plane; typically the horizontal axis.

x-intercept: The value of x at the point where a line or graph intersects the x-axis. The value of y is zero (0) at this point.

y-axis: One of two intersecting straight (number) lines that determine a coordinate system in a plane; typically the vertical axis.

y-intercept: The value of y at the point where a line or graph intersects the y-axis. The value of x is zero (0) at this point.

zero property: This property states that in addition the sum of a given number and zero is equal to the given number. In multiplication, the product of zero and any number is zero. For example, for any number a, in addition: $a + 0 = a$; in multiplication: $a \times 0 = 0$.

Mathematics Tutorial

Directions:

Today you will be taking the Ohio Grade 6 Mathematics Achievement Test. Three different types of questions appear on this test: multiple choice, short answer and extended response.

There are several important things to remember:

1. Read each question carefully. Think about what is being asked. Look carefully at graphs or diagrams because they will help you understand the question.

2. You may use the blank areas of your Student Test Booklet to solve problems. You may also use the optional grid paper in the answer document to solve problems.

3. For short-answer and extended-response questions, use a pencil to write your answers neatly and clearly in the gridded space provided in the answer document. Any answers you write in the Student Test Booklet will not be scored.

4. Short-answer questions are worth two points. Extended-response questions are worth four points. Point values are printed near each question in your Student Test Booklet. The amount of gridded space provided for your answers is the same for all two- and four-point questions.

5. For multiple-choice questions, shade in the circle next to your choice in the answer document for the test question. Mark only one choice for each question. Darken completely the circles on the answer document. If you change an answer, make sure that you erase your old answer completely.

6. Do not spend too much time on one question. Go on to the next question and return to the question skipped after answering the remaining questions.

7. Check over your work when you are finished.

Go to next page

*Question **1** assesses:*

Number, Number Sense and Operations Standard

Benchmark C: Develop meaning for percents, including percents greater than 100 and less than 1.

4. Describe what it means to find a specific percent of a number, using real-life examples.

Mathematics **M**

1. Ivy and her family celebrated her birthday at her favorite Mexican restaurant. The bill came to $39.00. Since the food and service were excellent, Ivy's dad wanted to leave a 20% tip.

    How much did he leave?

    A. $3.90

    B. $7.80

    C. $9.75

    D. $11.70

    Go to next page ▶

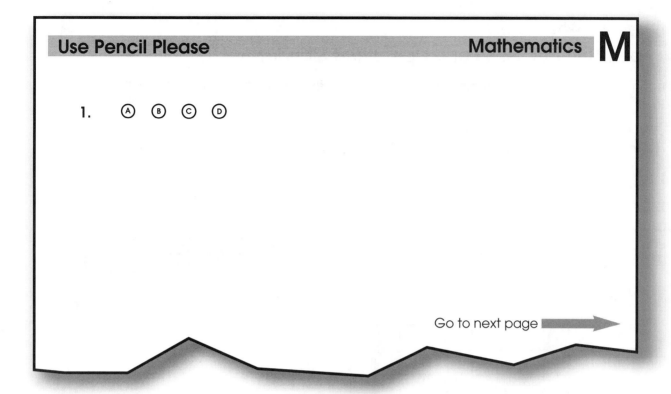

Use Pencil Please

Mathematics M

1. Ⓐ Ⓑ Ⓒ Ⓓ

Go to next page ➡

Analysis: *The correct answer is Choice B. To find 20% of $39.00, multiply 0.20 x $39.00 = $7.80. Choice A is not correct because $3.90 is 10% of $39.00. Choice C is not correct because $9.75 is 25% of $39.00. Choice D is not correct because $11.70 is 30% of $39.00.*

Question **2** *assesses:*

Number, Number Sense and Operations Standard

Benchmark C: Develop meaning for percents, including percents greater than 100 and less than 1.

5. Use models and pictures to relate concepts of ratio, proportion and percent, including percents less than 1 and greater than 100.

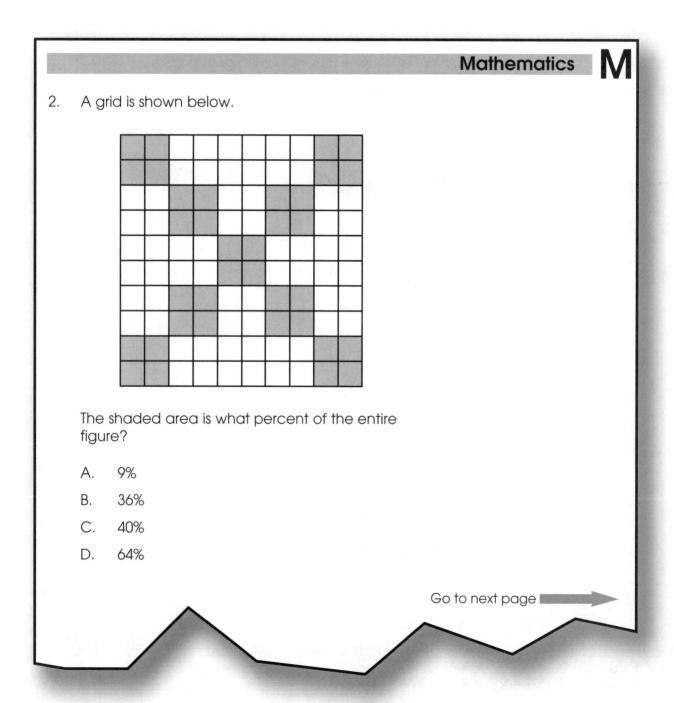

Mathematics **M**

2. A grid is shown below.

The shaded area is what percent of the entire figure?

A. 9%

B. 36%

C. 40%

D. 64%

Go to next page ➡

       © Englefield & Associates, Inc.

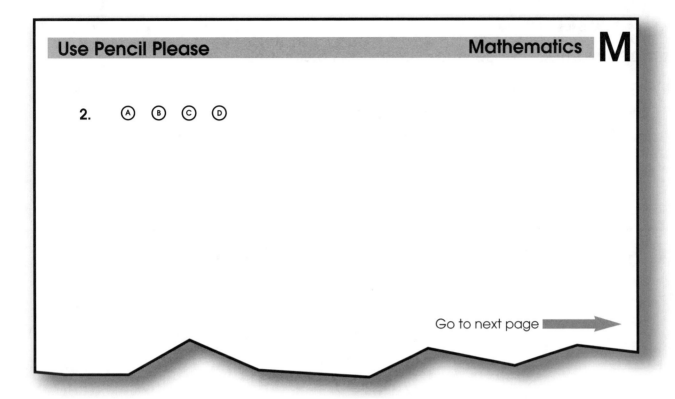

Use Pencil Please   **Mathematics** **M**

2.   Ⓐ   Ⓑ   Ⓒ   Ⓓ

Go to next page ➤

Analysis: *The correct answer is Choice B. Thirty-six of the one-hundred grid squares are shaded, so 36% are shaded. Choice A is incorrect because it is a distractor; there appears to be nine shaded boxes on the grid, but it is actually 36 shaded boxes. Choice C is not correct because it is an approximation, not an exact answer. Choice D is not correct because it is the percent of squares unshaded.*

Question **3** *assesses:*

Number, Number Sense and Operations Standard

Benchmark D: Use models and pictures to relate concepts of ratio, proportion and percent.

3. Explain why a number is referred to as being "rational," and recognize that the expression *a/b* can mean *a* parts of size 1/*b* each, *a* divided by *b*, or the ratio of *a* to *b*.

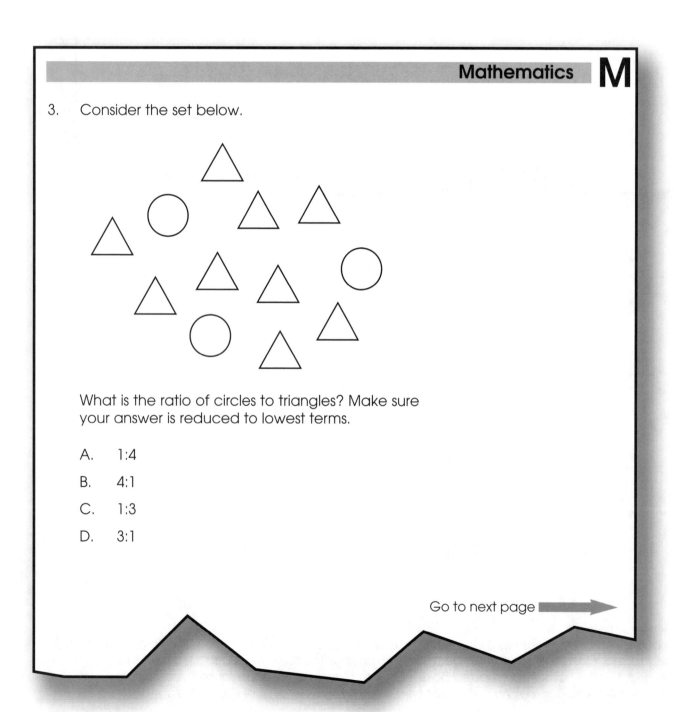

Mathematics **M**

3.   Consider the set below.

What is the ratio of circles to triangles? Make sure your answer is reduced to lowest terms.

A.   1:4

B.   4:1

C.   1:3

D.   3:1

Go to next page ➡

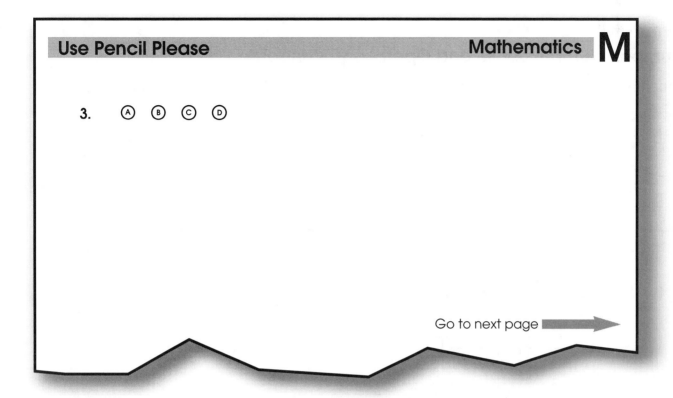

Mathematics **M**

3.   Ⓐ   Ⓑ   Ⓒ   Ⓓ

Go to next page ➤

Analysis: *The correct answer is Choice C. There are 3 circles and 9 triangles, so the ratio of circles to triangles is 3:9 which reduces to 1:3. Choice A is incorrect because its ratio is the number to circles to the number of total objects, 3:12 which reduces to 1:4. Choice B is incorrect because its ratio is the number of total objects to the number of circles. Choice D is incorrect because its ratio is the number of triangles to the nnumber of circles, 9:3 which reduces to 3:1.*

Question **4** *assesses:*

Number, Number Sense and Operations Standard

Benchmark D: Use models and pictures to relate concepts of ratio, proportion and percent.

5. Use models and pictures to relate concepts of ratio, proportion and percent, including percents less than 1 and greater than 100.

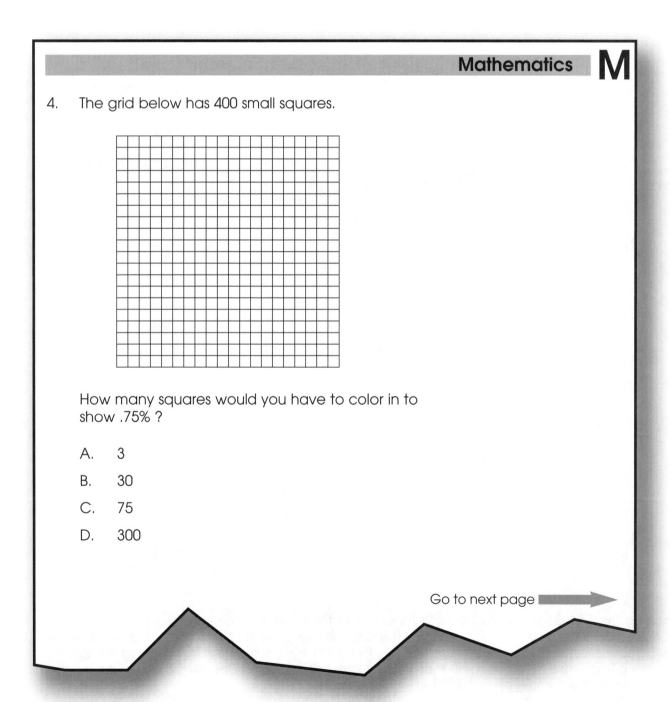

Mathematics **M**

4.   The grid below has 400 small squares.

How many squares would you have to color in to show .75% ?

A.   3

B.   30

C.   75

D.   300

Go to next page ➡

© Englefield & Associates, Inc.

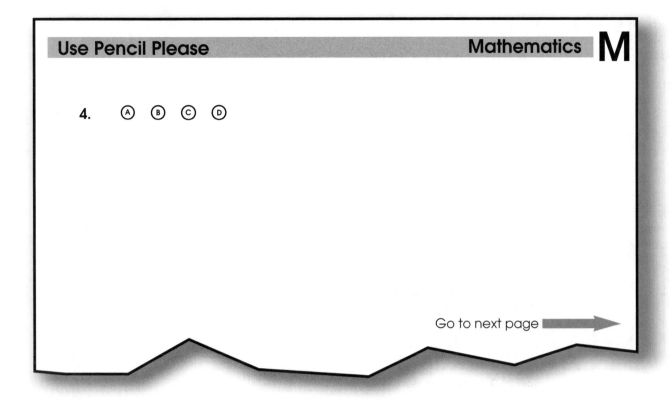

Use Pencil Please

Mathematics M

4. Ⓐ Ⓑ Ⓒ Ⓓ

Go to next page ➡

Analysis: The correct answer is Choice A. Be very careful converting percents to decimals especially when the percent is less than one. In the above problem, .75% of 400 = .0075 x 400 = 3. Choice B appears to be a guess and is incorrect. Choice C is also a guess based on the numerals in the given percent. Choice C is incorrect. Choice D is incorrect since 300 is 75% of 400, not .75%. Notice that 75% divided by 100 equals .75% and 300 divided by 100 equals 3, the correct answer.

Question **5** *assesses:*

Number, Number Sense and Operations Standard

Benchmark D: Use models and pictures to relate concepts of ratio, proportion and percent.

9. Give examples of how ratios are used to represent comparisons; e.g., part-to-part, part-to-whole, whole-to-part.

Mathematics

5. Sarah found the recipe below for Special Oatmeal Cookies. She wants to make as many of these cookies as possible and has plenty of each ingredient except for flour of which she only has 7 cups left.

Special Oatmeal Cookies

2 cups all purpose flour	1 teaspoon baking powder
1 teaspoon ground cinnamon	1/2 teaspoon baking soda
1/2 teaspoon salt	3/4 cup (1 1/2 sticks) unsalted butter
1/4 cup solid vegetable shortening	1 cup sugar
1 cup (packed) dark brown sugar	1/4 cup honey
2 large eggs	1 tablespoon vanilla extract
3 cups old-fashioned oatmeal	1 cup raisins
1 cup chopped pitted dates	1 cup chopped walnuts

If she decides to use all of her flour, how many cups of old-fashioned oatmeal will Sarah need to keep the recipe in proportion?

A. $\frac{6}{7}$ cup

B. $4\frac{1}{2}$ cups

C. 9 cups

D. $10\frac{1}{2}$ cups

Go to next page ▶

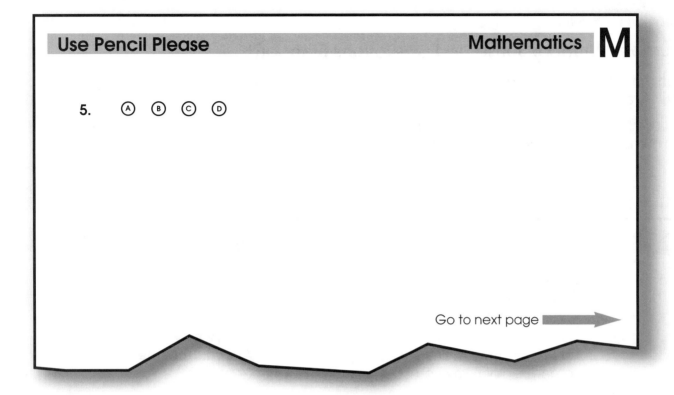

Use Pencil Please　　　　　　　　　　　　**Mathematics** **M**

5.　ⓐ　ⓑ　ⓒ　ⓓ

Go to next page ➡

Analysis: *The correct answer is Choice D. The easiest way to solve this problem is with a proportion. The important thing to remember is to keep the information in the two fractions in the same order. For example, in this problem if one fraction is:* $\frac{\text{flour in recipe}}{\text{flour actually used}}$ *the other fraction has to be:* $\frac{\text{oatmeal in recipe}}{\text{oatmeal actually used}}$. *The second fraction cannot be flipped upside down. So,* $\frac{2}{7} = \frac{3}{x}$. *Cross-multiplying yields 2x =21, so x = 10.5 or* $10\frac{1}{2}$ *cups of oatmeal. Choice A could not possibly be correct because it calls for less oatmeal than the original recipe when it should call for more. It results from mixing the numerators and the denominators of the equivalent fractions in the wrong order. This has also been done in Choice B and it is also incorrect. Choice C is incorrect; it appears to be an approximation based on tripling the ingredients. It might be OK for an estimate, but Choice D is a better answer.*

Question 6 assesses:

Number, Number Sense and Operations Standard

Benchmark E: Use order of operations, including use of parenthesis and exponents to solve multi-step problems, and verify and interpret the results.

6. Use the order of operations, including the use of exponents, decimals and rational numbers, to simplify numerical expressions.

Mathematics **M**

6. Look at the expression below.

$$5 \times (6 - 4)^2 + 3$$

In your **Answer Document**, simplify this expression. List each step and explain why you completed each step in the order you've listed.

For question 6, respond completely in your **Answer Document**. (4 points)

Go to next page ➡

Copying is Prohibited   © Englefield & Associates, Inc.

Use Pencil Please
Mathematics M

6. Write your response to question 6 in the space below.

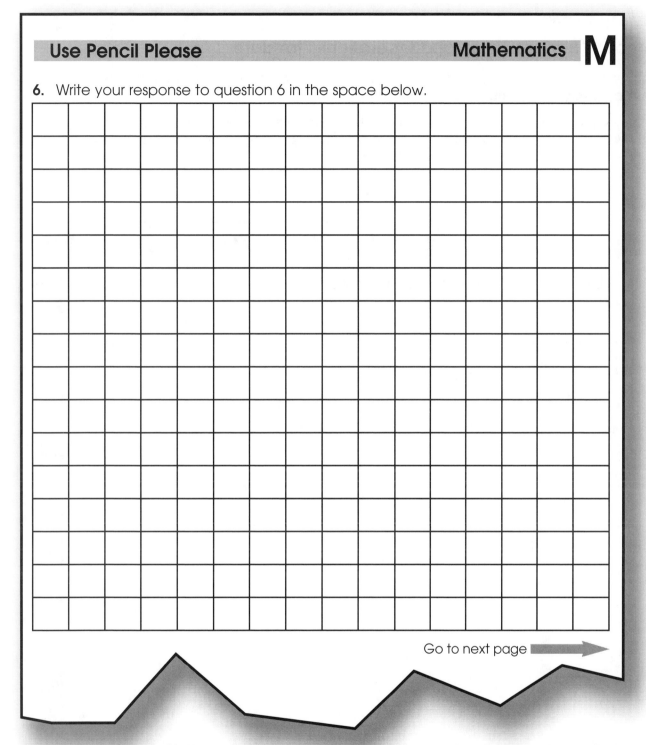

Go to next page ➡

Analysis: The answer is 23. When simplifying an expression with several mathematical operations, each must be completed in its proper order. This order can easily be remembered by referring to the word PEMDAS. The P in PEMDAS stands for parentheses, so the first operation is 6 – 4 = 2. The expression is now 5 x 2² + 3. The E in PEMDAS stands for exponent, so the next operation is 2² = 4. The expression is now 5 x 4 + 3. The M in PEMDAS stands for multiplication, so the next operation is 5 x 4 = 20. The expression is now 20 + 3. The D in PEMDAS stands for division, but there are no divisions in this expression. The A in PEMDAS stands for addition, so the expression is completed with 20 + 3 = 23. The S in PEMDAS stands for subtraction, but there are no subtractions left to complete in this expression.

Question **7** *assesses:*

Number, Number Sense and Operations Standard

Benchmark G: Apply and explain the use of prime factorizations, common factors, and common multiples in problem situations.

1. Decompose and recompose whole numbers using factors and exponents (e.g., $32 = 2 \times 2 \times 2 \times 2 \times 2 = 2^5$), and explain why "squared" means "second power" and "cubed" means "third power."

Mathematics M

7. The correct way to factor the number 300 down to prime factors is:

    A. $3 \times 4 \times 5^2$

    B. $2^2 \times 3^2 \times 5^2$

    C. $2^2 \times 3 \times 5^2$

    D. $2^2 \times 3 \times 25$

Go to next page

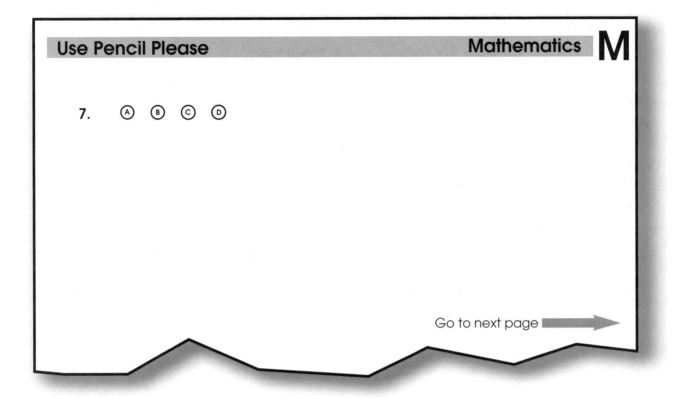

7. Ⓐ Ⓑ Ⓒ Ⓓ

Go to next page ▶

Analysis: *The correct answer is Choice C. A prime number has only two factors, itself and one. The expression in Choice C could be written as: 2 x 2 x 3 x 5 x 5. All of these factors are primes and their product is 300. Choice A is incorrect because 4 is listed as a factor, but it is not a prime factor. Choice B is incorrect because the product of these factors is 900, not 300. Choice D is incorrect because 25 is listed as a factor, but it is not a prime number.*

Question **8** *assesses:*

Number, Number Sense and Operations Standard

Benchmark G: Apply and explain the use of prime factorizations, common factors, and common multiples in problem situations.

2. Find and use the prime factorization of composite numbers. For example:
   a. Use the prime factorization to recognize the greatest common factor (GCF).
   b. Use the prime factorization to recognize the least common multiple (LCM).
   c. Apply the prime factorization to solve problems and explain.

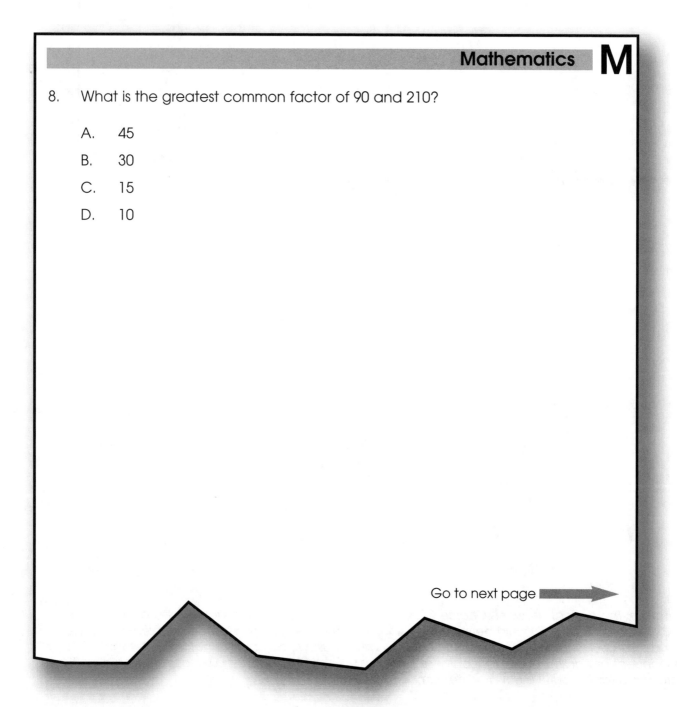

Mathematics **M**

8. What is the greatest common factor of 90 and 210?

    A. 45

    B. 30

    C. 15

    D. 10

Go to next page ▬▬►

Use Pencil Please **Mathematics** **M**

8. Ⓐ Ⓑ Ⓒ Ⓓ

Go to next page ➡

Analysis: The correct answer is Choice B. To solve this problem, you can try dividing each of your answer choices into given numbers and choose the largest one which evenly divides them, or you can factor each number down to prime factors and find the product of all the factors that they have in common. For example, the tree diagrams below show 90 and 210 factored down to primes.

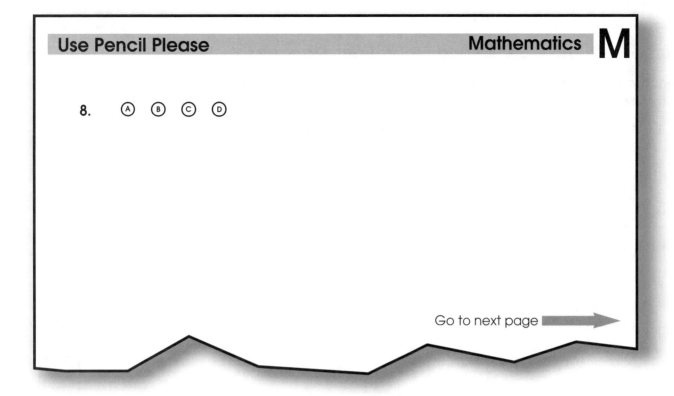

$$90 = 2 \times 3 \times 3 \times 5$$

$$210 = 2 \times 3 \times 5 \times 7$$

As you can see, the diagram has one 2, one 3, and one 5 in common, therefore the greatest common factor of these two numbers is 2 x 3 x 5 = 30. Choice A is incorrect because 45 is not a factor of 210 since it doesn't divide into 210 evenly. Choices C and D are incorrect because although they are common factors of 90 and 210, they are not the greatest factor.

Question 9 assesses:

Number, Number Sense and Operations Standard

Benchmark H: Use and analyze the steps in standard and non-standard algorithms for computing with fractions, decimals and integers.

8. Represent multiplication and division situations involving fractions and decimals with models and visual representations; e.g., show with pattern blocks what it means to take 2 2/3 ÷ 1/6.

Mathematics **M**

9. The grid shown below represents an operation performed with two fractions. The darkest shaded portion represents the answer.

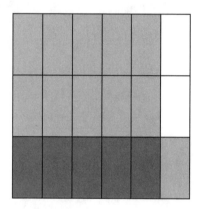

Which of the following operations could this grid represent?

A. $\frac{1}{3} \times \frac{1}{6}$

B. $\frac{2}{3} \times \frac{3}{6}$

C. $\frac{5}{6} \div \frac{1}{3}$

D. $\frac{5}{6} \times \frac{1}{3}$

Go to next page ➡

Copying is Prohibited
© Englefield & Associates, Inc.

Use Pencil Please

Mathematics M

9. Ⓐ Ⓑ Ⓒ Ⓓ

Go to next page ➡

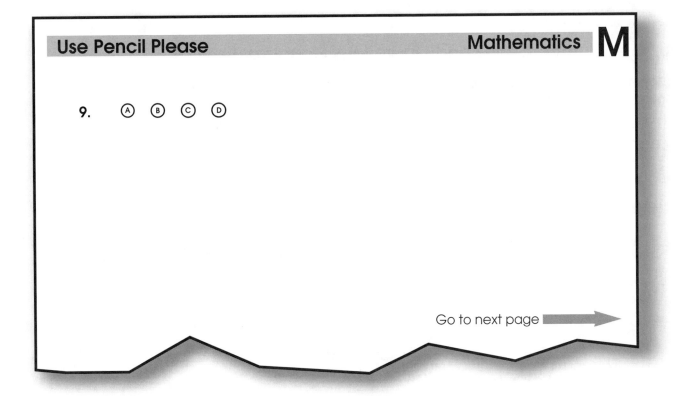

Analysis: *The correct answer is Choice D. The figure is cut into 6 columns of which 5 are shaded. This represents the fraction 5/6. The figure is also cut into 3 rows of which 1 is shaded. This represents the fraction 1/3. The double-shaded cells (where the shaded columns and rows overlap) represent the answer. There are 5 double-shaded cells out of 18 cells in all, so this represents the fraction 5/18. Notice that in Choice D, 5/6 x 1/3 = 5/18. Choice A is incorrect because 1/3 x 1/6 = 1/18, not 5/18 as represented in the figure. Choice B is incorrect because 2/3 x 3/6 = 6/18 = 1/3, not 5/18 as represented in the figure. Choice C is incorrect because 5/6 ÷ 1/3 = 5/6 x 3/1 = 15/6, not 5/18 as represented in the figure.*

Question **10** *assesses:*

Number, Number Sense and Operations Standard

Benchmark H: Use and analyze the steps in standard and non-standard algorithms for computing with fractions, decimals and integers.

12. Develop and analyze algorithms for computing with fractions and decimals, and demonstrate fluency in their use.

10. The models below represent two different fractions.

$\frac{3}{5}$  =

$\frac{1}{4}$ 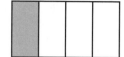 =

Which equation shows the sum of these two fractions?

A. $\frac{3}{5} + \frac{1}{4} = \frac{17}{20}$

B. $\frac{3}{5} + \frac{1}{4} = \frac{4}{20}$

C. $\frac{3}{5} + \frac{1}{4} = \frac{4}{9}$

D. $\frac{3}{5} + \frac{1}{4} = \frac{13}{20}$

Go to next page ➡

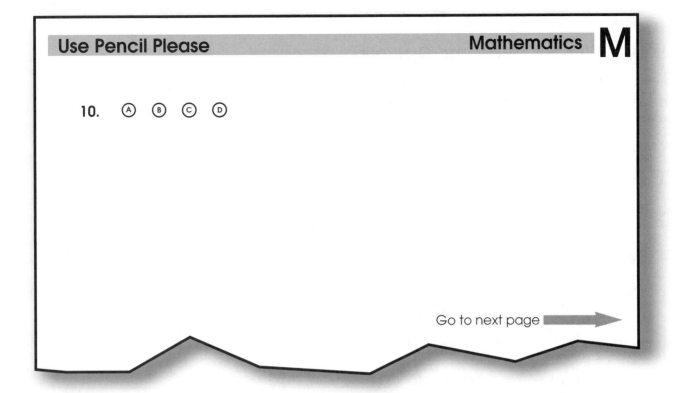

Use Pencil Please   **Mathematics** **M**

10.   Ⓐ   Ⓑ   Ⓒ   Ⓓ

Go to next page ➡

Analysis: *The correct answer is Choice A. In order to add two fractions with different denominators you must first find a common denominator. The lowest common denominator of 5 and 4 is 20. Remember that if you multiply a number by one, you do not change the value of the number. To put both fractions into twentieths, multiply each by a special version of one.*

$$\frac{3}{5} \times \frac{4}{4} = \frac{12}{20}$$

$$+ \frac{1}{4} \times \frac{5}{5} = + \frac{5}{20}$$

$$\frac{17}{20}$$

Notice that $\frac{3}{5}$ is multiplied by $\frac{4}{4}$ which is a special version of 1 since any number over itself is 1. This changes $\frac{3}{5}$ to $\frac{12}{20}$ without changing its value. Also notice that $\frac{1}{4}$ is multiplied by $\frac{5}{5}$ to change it to $\frac{5}{20}$ without changing its value. Choice B is incorrect because only the denominators of the fractions have been changed to twentieths. The numerators were not changed, so the new fractions are not equivalent to the old. Choice C is incorrect because both the numerators and the denominators were added without trying to find a common denominator. Choice D is incorrect because only the first fraction was correctly converted to an equivalent fraction in twentieths.

Question **11** *assesses:*

Number, Number Sense and Operations Standard

Benchmark I: Use a variety of strategies, including proportional reasoning, to estimate, compute, solve and explain solutions to problems involving integers, fractions, decimals and percents.

7. Use simple expressions involving integers to represent and solve problems; e.g., if a running back loses 15 yards on the first carry but gains 8 yards on the second carry, what is the net gain/loss?

Mathematics **M**

11. On Monday, the temperature at noon was 78° F. By 4:00 p.m. the temperature had risen 13°, but by 6:00 p.m. it had cooled by 5°. By midnight the temperature had fallen another 16°.

    Which expression can be used to find the temperature at midnight?

    A.   78 + 13 – 5 + 16

    B.   78 + 13 – 5 – 16

    C.   78 – 13 – 5 – 16

    D.   78 + 13 + 5 – 16

Go to next page ➡

Copying is Prohibited   © Englefield & Associates, Inc.

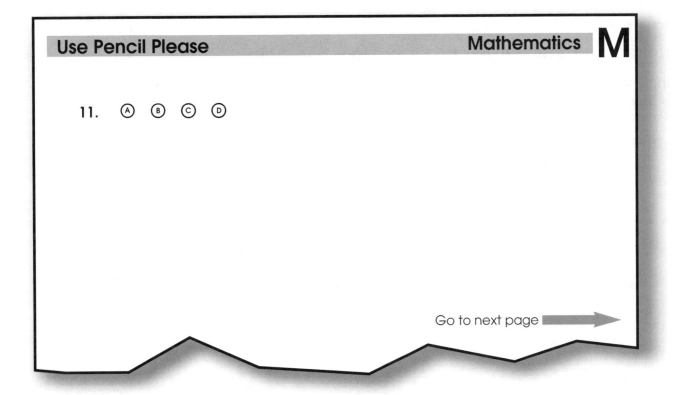

Go to next page ▶

Analysis: *The correct answer is Choice B. The words "risen" or "warmed up" mean adding degrees. The words "fallen" or "cooled off" mean subtracting degrees. All answer choices start with 78°. This is the correct starting temperature. Since the temperature at 4:00 p.m. had risen 13°, you must add 13. This eliminates Choice C which subtracts 13. By 6:00 p.m. the temperature had cooled off by 5° so you should subtract 5. This eliminates Choice D which adds 5. Finally, by midnight the temperature had fallen another 16°, so 16 should be subtracted. This eliminates Choice A which adds 16.*

Question **12** *assesses:*

Number, Number Sense and Operations Standard

Benchmark I: Use a variety of strategies, including proportional reasoning, to estimate, compute, solve and explain solutions to problems involving integers, fractions, decimals and percents.

11. Perform fraction and decimal computations and justify their solutions; e.g., using manipulatives, diagrams, mathematical reasoning.

Mathematics **M**

12. Carey's class had a pizza party. The pictures below show how much pizza was left over.

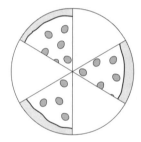 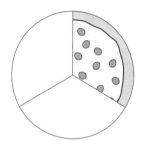

For question 12, respond completely in your **Answer Document**. (2 points)

In your **Answer Document**, express the total amount of pizza left over as a reduced fraction of a whole pizza. Justify your answer.

Go to next page ➡

Copying is Prohibited

© Englefield & Associates, Inc.

Use Pencil Please   Mathematics **M**

12. Write your response to question 12 in the space below.

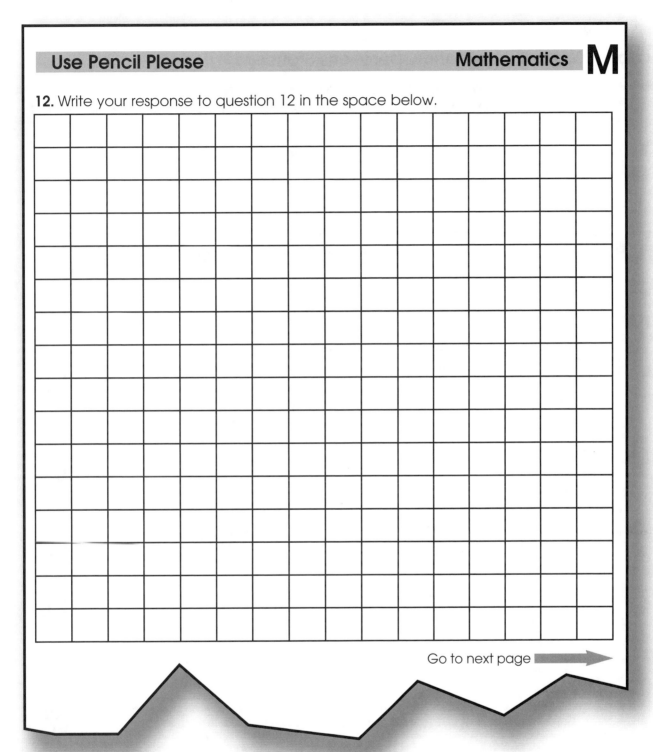

Go to next page ▶

Analysis: *The answer is 5/6. This problem calls for adding fractions with two different denominators. The pizza on the left has 3 pieces out of 6 left over. The pizza on the right has 1 piece out of 3 left over. Expressed as fractions, these amounts are 3/6 and 1/3. To add these fractions we must have a common denominator. The lowest common multiple of 6 and 3 is 6. The first fraction is already in sixths, so if we change 1/3 to sixths we will be able to add the fractions. Remember that you can always multiply any number by one without changing the value of the number. In this case, we will multiply 1/3 by a special form of one, 2/2, which will change 1/3 to 2/6 without changing its value.*

$$\frac{3}{6} \longrightarrow \frac{3}{6}$$

$$+\frac{1}{3} \times \frac{2}{2} = +\frac{2}{6}$$

$$\frac{5}{6}$$

Question **13** *assesses:*

Number, Number Sense and Operations Standard

Benchmark I: Use a variety of strategies, including proportional reasoning, to estimate, compute, solve and explain solutions to problems involving integers, fractions, decimals and percents.

13. Estimate reasonable solutions to problem situations involving fractions and decimals; e.g., 7/8 + 12/13 ≈ 2 and 4.23 x 5.8 ≈ 25.

Mathematics M

13. The White Star Line's RMS Titanic, weighing 46,328 tons, was the largest ocean liner ever built when it was completed on March 31, 1912. Currently, the largest ocean liner in the world is Cunard's Queen Mary 2 which weighs 151,400 tons.

Approximately, how many times heavier than the Titanic is the Queen Mary 2?

A. 2

B. 3

C. 4

D. 5

Go to next page ➡

Copying is Prohibited

© Englefield & Associates, Inc.

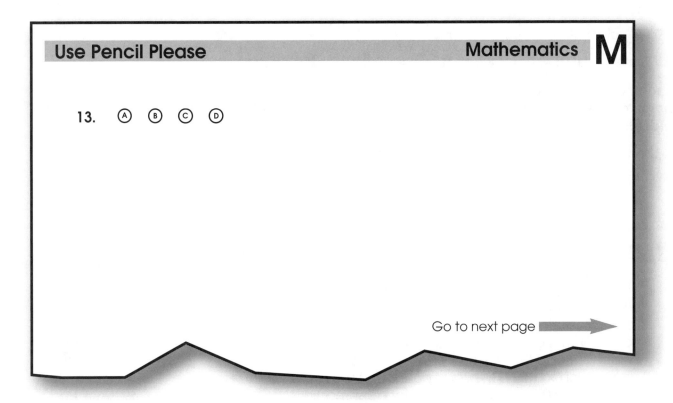

Mathematics M

13.   Ⓐ   Ⓑ   Ⓒ   Ⓓ

Go to next page ▶

Analysis: *The correct answer is Choice B. Rounding both ships' weights to the nearest 10,000 tons yields about 50,000 tons for Titanic and about 150,000 tons for the Queen Mary 2. Dividing 150,000 by 50,000 gives an answer of 3, so the Queen Mary 2 is about three times as heavy as the Titanic.*

Question **14** *assesses:*

Number, Number Sense and Operations Standard

Benchmark I: Use a variety of strategies, including proportional reasoning, to estimate, compute, solve and explain solutions to problems involving integers, fractions, decimals and percents.

14. Use proportional reasoning, ratios and percents to represent problem situations and determine the reasonableness of solutions.

Mathematics	**M**

14. A toy company wants to make a plastic model of a newly discovered dinosaur named *sauroposeidon*, the tallest dinosaur ever found. The company already makes a 4-inch model of an African elephant and they want their new model to be in proportion to this. If the *sauroposeidon* they are copying is 60 feet tall and their elephant model is based on an animal 13 feet tall, how tall must their new dinosaur model be?

For question 14, respond completely in your **Answer Document**. (2 points)

In your **Answer Document**, round you answer to the nearest tenth of an inch.

Go to next page ▶

Copying is Prohibited   © Englefield & Associates, Inc.

Use Pencil Please

Mathematics **M**

14. Write your response to question 14 in the space below.

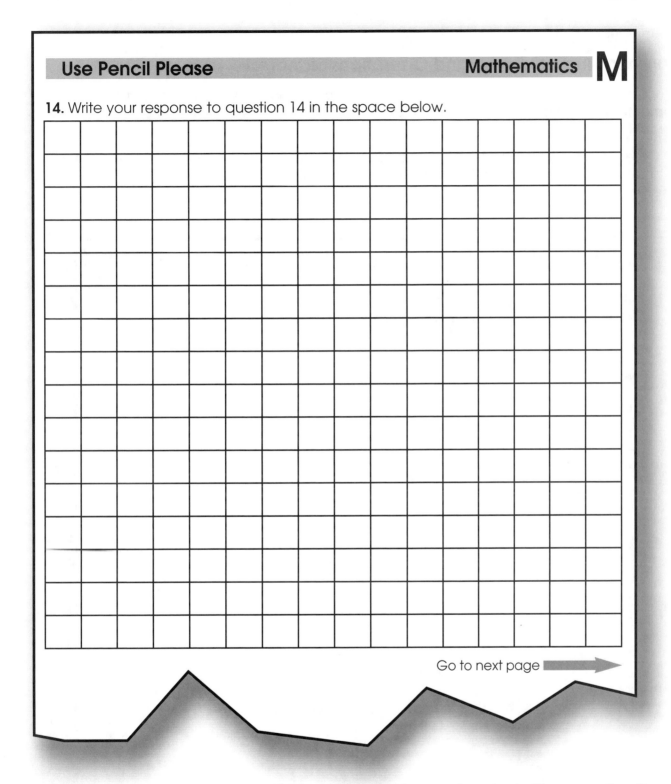

Go to next page ➡

Analysis: *The correct answer is about 18.5 inches. This problem can be solved with a proportion. The ratio of the dinosaur's height to the elephant's height (60/13) is the same as the model dinosaur's height to the model elephant's height (h/4). Since we are trying to find the height of the dinosaur model, it is the unknown, and is represented by a variable, say h:* $\frac{60}{13} = \frac{h}{4}$. *Cross multiplying:* $13h = 240$; $h \approx 18.462 \approx 18.5$ *inches.*

Question **15** *assesses:*

Number, Number Sense and Operations Standard

Benchmark I: Use a variety of strategies, including proportional reasoning, to estimate, compute, solve and explain solutions to problems involving integers, fractions, decimals and percents.

15. Determine the percent of a number and solve related problems; e.g., find the percent markdown if the original price was $140, and the sale price is $100.

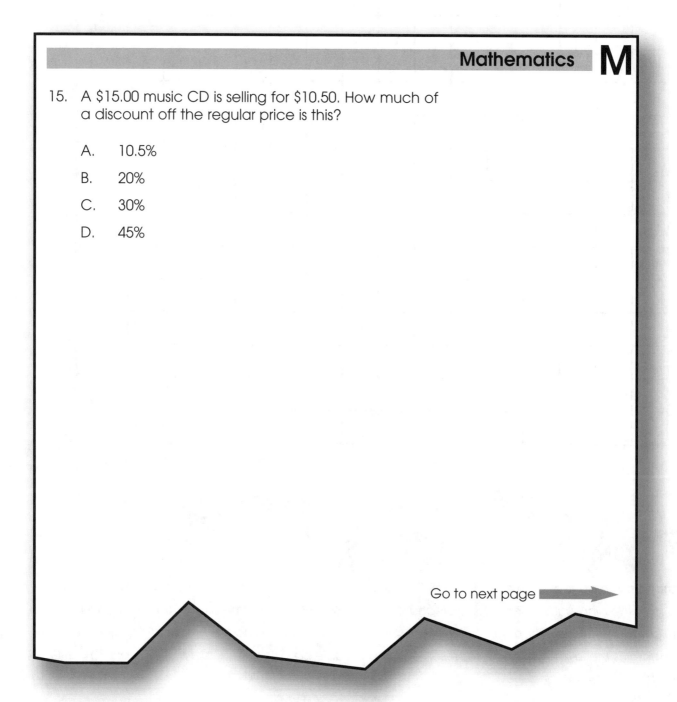

Mathematics **M**

15. A $15.00 music CD is selling for $10.50. How much of a discount off the regular price is this?

    A.   10.5%

    B.   20%

    C.   30%

    D.   45%

Go to next page ➡

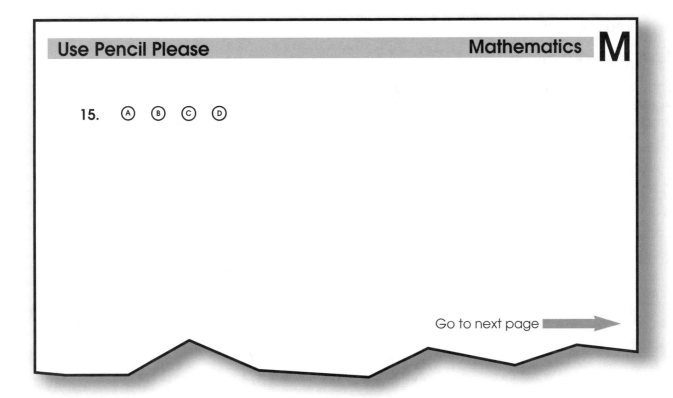

Use Pencil Please

Mathematics M

15. Ⓐ   Ⓑ   Ⓒ   Ⓓ

Go to next page ➡

Analysis: The correct answer is Choice C. The quickest way to solve this problem is to divide the sale price by the original price: 10.50 ÷ 15 = .7 = 70%. The 70% is the percentage of the original price represented by the sale price. In other words, $10.50 is 70% of $15.00. This means it is a 30% discount (100% – 70% = 30%). Choice A is incorrect because it is just the sales price rewritten as a percent. Choice B is just a guess and is incorrect. Choice D is incorrect because it is the dollar savings rewritten incorrectly as a percentage.

Question **16** *assesses:*

Measurement Standard

Benchmark C: Identify appropriate tools and apply appropriate techniques for measuring angles, perimeter or circumference and area of triangles, quadrilaterals, circles and composite shapes, and surface area and volume of prisms and cylinders.

2. Use strategies to develop formulas for finding circumference and area of circles, and to determine the area of sectors; e.g., 1/2 circle, 2/3 circle, 1/3 circle, 1/4 circle.

Mathematics **M**

16. The circular window below is made up of three identical panes.

What is the area of each pane? Round your answer to the nearest square inch.

A.   3,944 square inches

B.   1,256 square inches

C.   628 square inches

D.   419 square inches

Go to next page ▶

Copying is Prohibited   © Englefield & Associates, Inc.

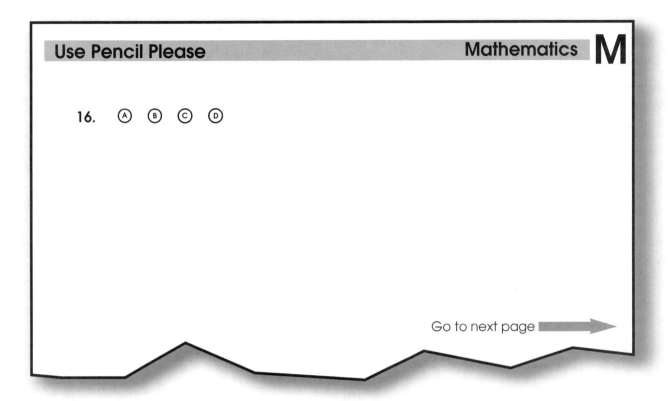

Use Pencil Please   **Mathematics** M

16. Ⓐ Ⓑ Ⓒ Ⓓ

Go to next page →

Analysis: *The correct answer is Choice D. The formula for the area of a circle is $A = \pi r^2$. The radius of this circle is 20 inches so its entire area is $A = \pi r^2$; $A = \pi(20)^2$; $A = 400\pi$; $A \approx 1256$. The problem asked us to find the area of each identical pane and since there are three, this area should be divided by three. $(1256 \div 3 \approx 419)$. Choice A is incorrect because it uses the formula $A = (\pi r)^2$, not $A = \pi r^2$. That is, it multiplies the radius times pi and then squares the result instead of squaring the radius first and then multiplying by pi. Choice B is incorrect because it is the area of the entire circle, not one of the panes. Choice C is incorrect because it is the area of half the entire circle, not one-third of it.*

Question 17 assesses:

Measurement Standard

Benchmark C: Identify appropriate tools and apply appropriate techniques for measuring angles, perimeter or circumference and area of triangles, quadrilaterals, circles and composite shapes, and surface area and volume of prisms and cylinders.

3. Estimate perimeter or circumference and area for circles, triangles and quadrilaterals, and surface area and volume for prisms and cylinders by:
   a. estimating lengths using string or links, areas using tiles or grid, and volumes using cubes;
   b. measuring attributes (diameter, side lengths, or heights) and using established formulas for circles, triangles, rectangles, parallelograms and rectangular prisms.

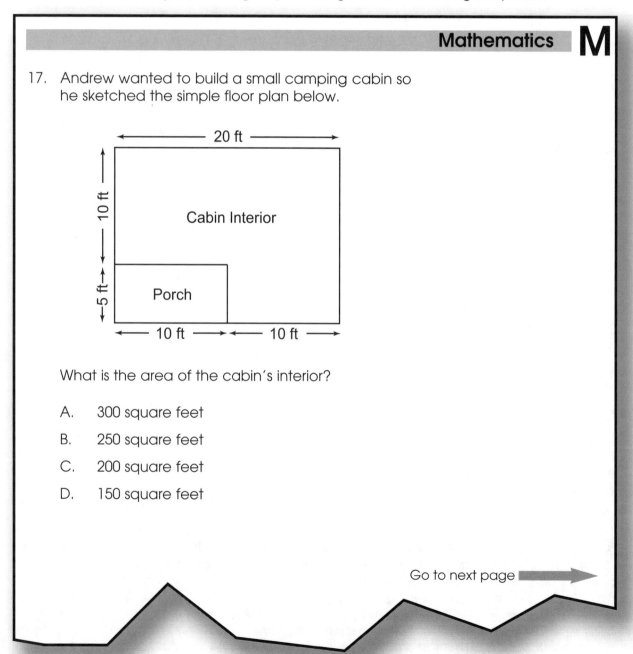

Mathematics **M**

17. Andrew wanted to build a small camping cabin so he sketched the simple floor plan below.

What is the area of the cabin's interior?

A.   300 square feet

B.   250 square feet

C.   200 square feet

D.   150 square feet

Go to next page ▶

Copying is Prohibited   © Englefield & Associates, Inc.

Use Pencil Please

Mathematics M

17.   Ⓐ   Ⓑ   Ⓒ   Ⓓ

Go to next page ➡

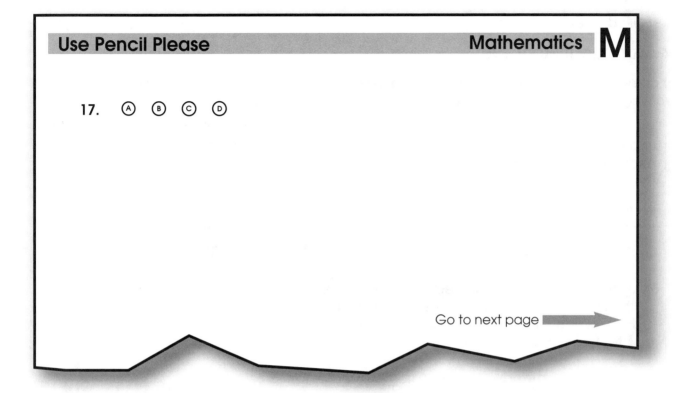

Analysis: *The correct answer is Choice B. The cabin's interior can be divided into a 10 ft x 10 ft square and a 10 ft x 15 ft rectangle as shown in the diagram at the right. This makes the interior 250 square feet (10 x 10 + 10 x 15 = 100 + 150 = 250). Choice A is incorrect because this is the area of the entire cabin including the porch. Choice C is incorrect because this is the area of only part of the cabin's interior as if the porch went all the way across the front of the cabin instead of only half-way across. Choice D is incorrect because this is half of the entire cabin's area when the interior is actually five-sixths of the total area.*

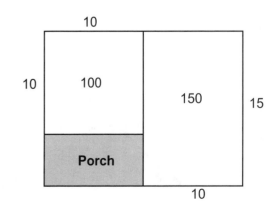

Question **18** *assesses:*

Measurement Standard

Benchmark E: Use problem solving techniques and technology as needed to solve problems involving length, weight, perimeter, area, volume, time and temperature.

4. Determine which measure (perimeter, area, surface area, volume) matches the context for a problem situation; e.g., perimeter is the context for fencing a garden, surface area is the context for painting a room.

Mathematics

18. Jimmy wants to paint his bedroom. The dimensions of the room are 14 feet by 16 feet with walls 8 feet high. He has one 3 feet by 7 feet door and two 3 feet by 4 feet windows in his room.

    What will Jimmy have to calculate first in order to buy the right amount of paint for his room?

    A. the perimeter of the room

    B. the volume of the room

    C. the surface area of the walls, floor, and ceiling

    D. the surface area of the walls, doors, and windows

Go to next page ➡

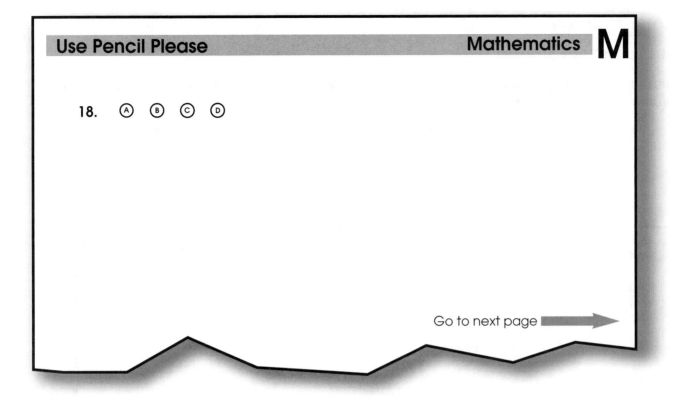

Use Pencil Please   **Mathematics** M

18.   Ⓐ   Ⓑ   Ⓒ   Ⓓ

Go to next page ➡

Analysis: *The correct answer is Choice D. Jimmy will need to calculate the surface area of the walls and subtract the surface area of the door and windows to get the total surface area to be painted. Choice A is incorrect because he does not need to calculate the perimeter of the room, since the perimeter does not consider the height of the walls. Choice B is incorrect because he does not need to calculate the volume of the room, since he is not filling the room with paint. Choice C is a possible answer, but it is not the best answer. Most people do not paint the floors of their bedrooms and they usually do not paint their ceilings the same color as the walls. Also, the doors and windows are not usually painted and Choice C does not consider them and is incorrect.*

Question **19** *assesses:*

Measurement Standard

Benchmark F: Analyze and explain what happens to area and perimeter or surface area and volume when the dimensions of an object are changed.

1. Understand and describe the difference between surface area and volume.

Mathematics **M**

19. The sketch below is the net of a rectangular prism (a box).

```
        ←  10 in  →
      ┌───────────┐
 3 in │           │ 3 in
   ┌──┼─ ─ ─ ─ ─ ─┼──┐
 6 │  │           │  │
 in│  │           │  │
   └──┼─ ─ ─ ─ ─ ─┼──┘
 3 in │           │
      │           │
 6 in │           │
      └───────────┘
        ←  10 in  →
```

Which of the follow statements is true?

A.   The volume of this box is 180 cubic inches.

B.   The surface area of this box is 180 square inches.

C.   The surface area of a box is the number of cubes of a certain size that will fit into it.

D.   The volume of a box is the amount of material measured in square units that it takes to construct the box's six faces.

Go to next page ▶

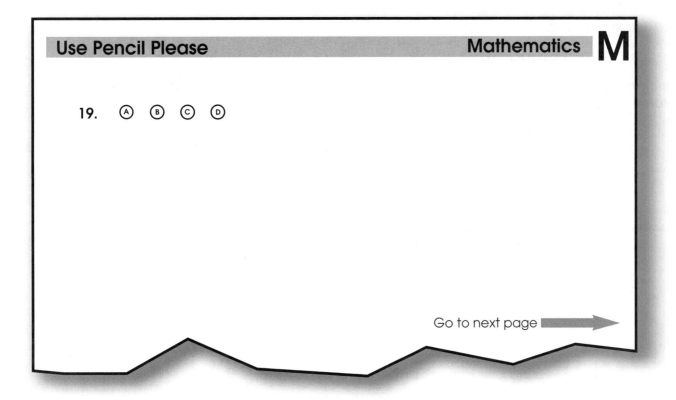

Use Pencil Please

Mathematics M

19. Ⓐ Ⓑ Ⓒ Ⓓ

Go to next page ➡

Analysis: The correct answer is Choice A. The volume of a box is the number of cubes of a certain size that will fit into it. Volume is calculated by multiplying the box's length by its width by its height. The volume of this box is 180 cubic inches (6 x 10 x 3). Choice B is incorrect because 180 is the box's volume, not its surface area. Choice C is incorrect because the given definition applies to volume, not surface area. Choice D is incorrect because the given definition applies to surface area, not volume.

Question **20** *assesses:*

Measurement Standard

Benchmark F: Analyze and explain what happens to area and perimeter or surface area and volume when the dimensions of an object are changed.

6. Describe what happens to the perimeter and area of a two-dimensional shape when the measurements of the shape are changed; e.g. length of sides are doubled.

Mathematics **M**

20. Heather has a 5 meter by 8 meter rectangular garden.

8 m

5 m

What will happen to its perimeter if she doubles the width and the length?

A.   The perimeter will triple.

B.   The perimeter will be multiplied by four.

C.   The perimeter will not change.

D.   The perimeter will double.

Go to next page ➡

© Englefield & Associates, Inc.

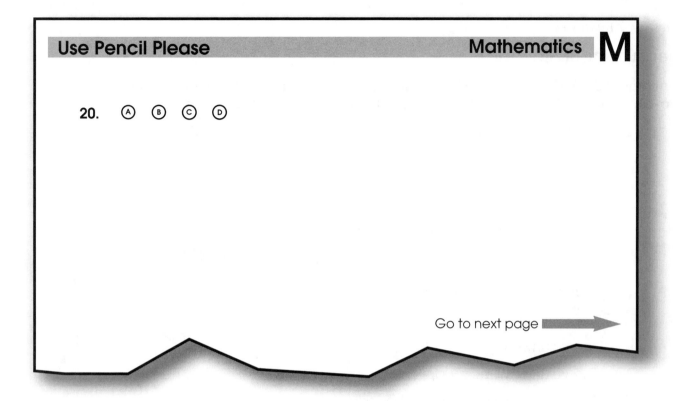

Use Pencil Please

Mathematics M

20. Ⓐ Ⓑ Ⓒ Ⓓ

Go to next page ▶

Analysis: *The correct answer is Choice D. The perimeter of the original garden is 5 + 5 + 8 + 8 = 26 meters. The perimeter of the enlarged garden is 10 + 10 + 16 + 16 = 52 meters. Since 52 is twice as big as 26, the perimeter doubles. Choice A is incorrect because the perimeter is doubled, not tripled. Choice B is incorrect because the perimeter of the enlarged garden will only double, not be multiplied by four. Choice C is incorrect because the perimeter will double and not remain the same.*

Question **21** *assesses:*

Measurement Standard

Benchmark G: Understand and demonstrate the independence of perimeter and area for two-dimensional shapes and of surface area and volume for three-dimensional shapes.

1. Understand and describe the difference between surface area and volume.

Mathematics **M**

21. What happens to the volume of a cube if each edge is doubled?

A. The volume will double.

B. The volume will be multiplied by four.

C. The volume will be multiplied by six.

D. The volume will be multiplied by eight.

Go to next page ➡

Tutorial

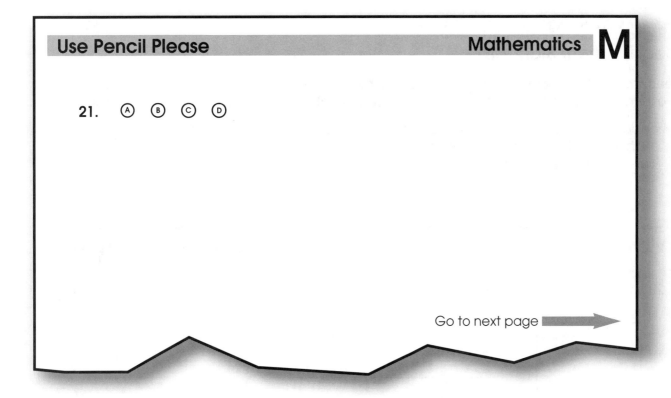

Use Pencil Please

Mathematics M

21. Ⓐ Ⓑ Ⓒ Ⓓ

Go to next page ➡

Analysis: *The correct answer is Choice D. The edges of the cube can be measured to determine the dimensions of the cube (length, width, and height). In order to simplify this problem start with a 1 x 1 x 1 cube. After each edge is doubled, the enlarged cube will have the dimensions 2 x 2 x 2. The volume of the original cube is 1 x 1 x 1 = 1 cubic unit. The area of the enlarged cube is 2 x 2 x 2 = 8 cubic units. Since 8 is eight times as large as 1, the volume is multiplied by eight. Choice A is incorrect because the volume is multiplied by eight, not doubled. Choice B is incorrect because the volume is multiplied by eight, not four. Choice C is incorrect because the volume is multiplied by eight, not six.*

*Question **22** assesses:*

Measurement Standard

Benchmark G: Understand and demonstrate the independence of perimeter and area for two-dimensional shapes and of surface area and volume for three-dimensional shapes.

5. Understand the difference between perimeter and area, and demonstrate that two shapes may have the same perimeter, but different areas or may have the same area, but different perimeters.

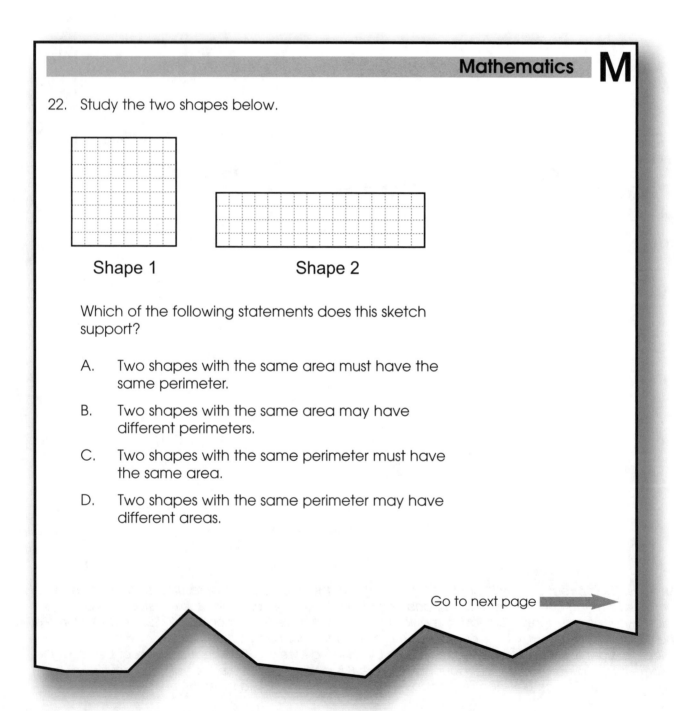

Mathematics **M**

22. Study the two shapes below.

Shape 1   Shape 2

Which of the following statements does this sketch support?

A. Two shapes with the same area must have the same perimeter.

B. Two shapes with the same area may have different perimeters.

C. Two shapes with the same perimeter must have the same area.

D. Two shapes with the same perimeter may have different areas.

Go to next page ➡

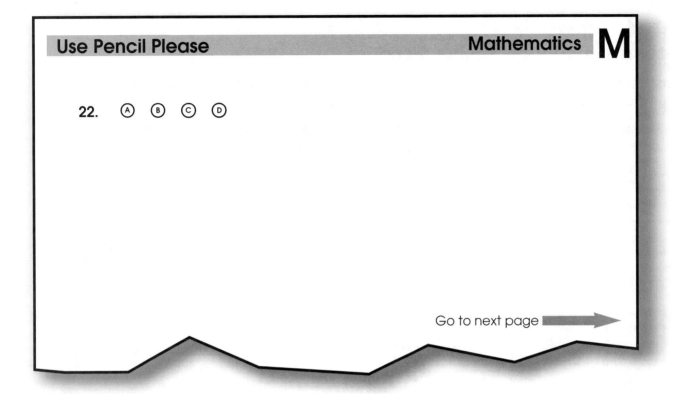

Go to next page ➡

Analysis: *The correct answer is Choice B. The area of Shape 1 is 64 square units (8 x 8) while its perimeter is 8 + 8 + 8 + 8 = 32 units. The area of Shape 2 is 64 square units (4 x 16) while its perimeter is 4 + 16 + 4 + 16 = 40 units. Thus, the shapes have the same area, but different perimeters. Choice A is incorrect because the two shapes do not have the same perimeter even though they have the same area. Choices C and D are incorrect because the two shapes do not have the same perimeter, so this sketch cannot support either of these choices. Choice D is true, but this statement is not supported by the sketches shown in the question.*

Question **23** *assesses:*

Geometry and Spatial Sense Standard

Benchmark D: Identify, describe and classify types of line pairs, angles, two-dimensional figures and three-dimensional objects using their properties.

1. Classify and describe two-dimensional and three-dimensional geometric figures and objects by using their properties; e.g., interior angle measures, perpendicular/parallel sides, congruent angles/sides.

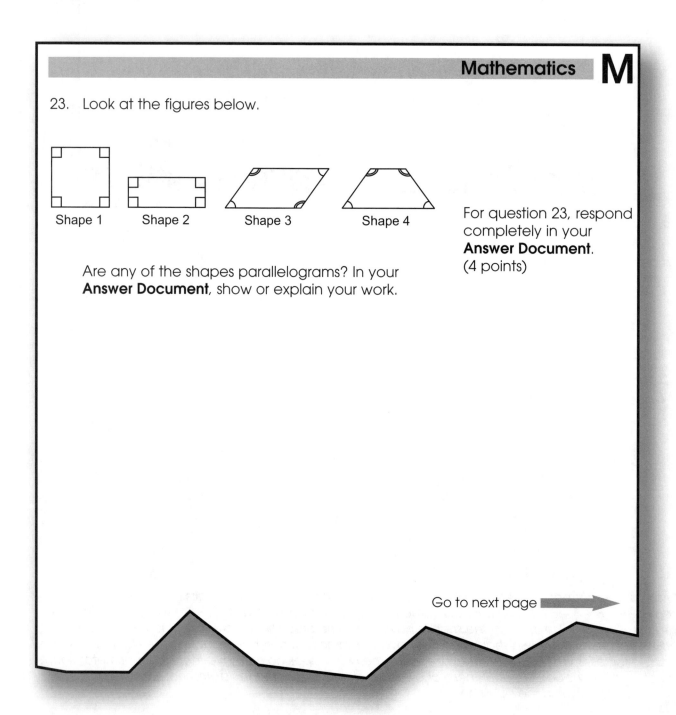

Mathematics **M**

23. Look at the figures below.

Shape 1   Shape 2   Shape 3   Shape 4

Are any of the shapes parallelograms? In your **Answer Document**, show or explain your work.

For question 23, respond completely in your **Answer Document**. (4 points)

Go to next page ➡

Use Pencil Please
Mathematics M

23. Write your response to question 23 in the space below.

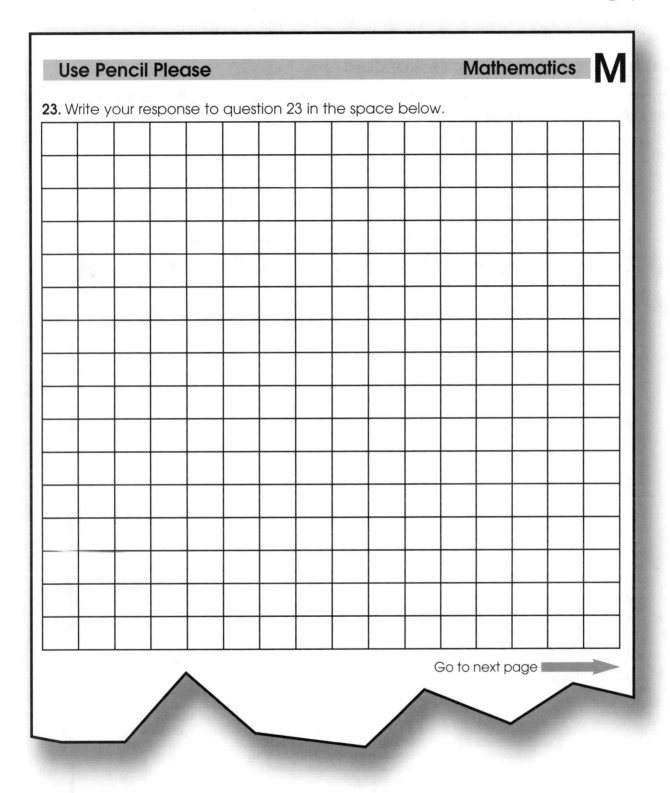

Go to next page ➡

Analysis: *Extended-response answers may vary. Parallelograms have two pair of parallel sides. They also have two pair of opposite congruent sides and two pair of opposite congruent angles. Shapes 1, 2 and 3 meet all of these requirements. Only Shape 4 does not meet any of them. A square, a rectangle, and a rhombus are also types of parallelograms. Shape 4 is a trapezoid. The usual definition of a trapezoid states that it must have only one pair of parallel sides.*

Question **24** *assesses:*

Geometry and Spatial Sense Standard

Benchmark D: Identify, describe and classify types of line pairs, angles, two-dimensional figures and three-dimensional objects using their properties.

2. Use standard language to define geometric vocabulary: vertex, face, altitude, diagonal, isosceles, equilateral, acute, obtuse and other vocabulary as appropriate.

Mathematics **M**

24. Which of the following describes the triangular prism below?

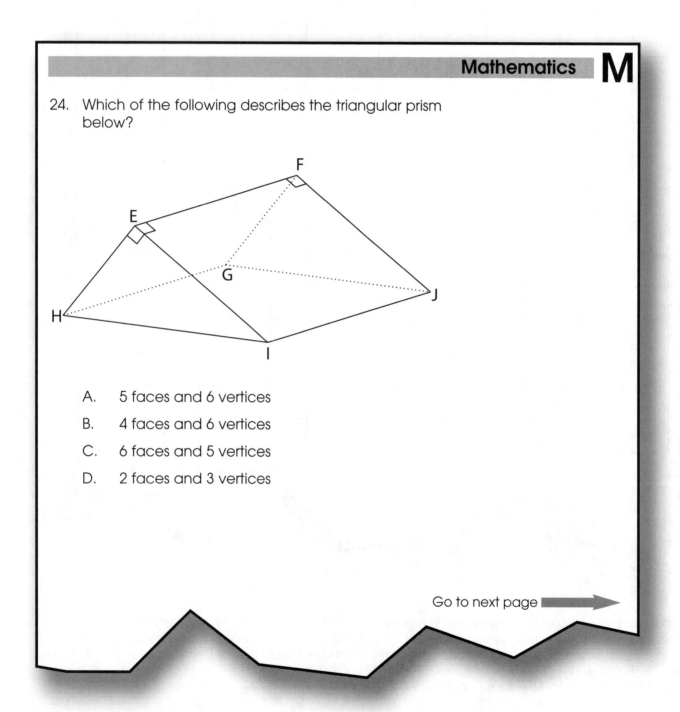

A.   5 faces and 6 vertices

B.   4 faces and 6 vertices

C.   6 faces and 5 vertices

D.   2 faces and 3 vertices

Go to next page ➡

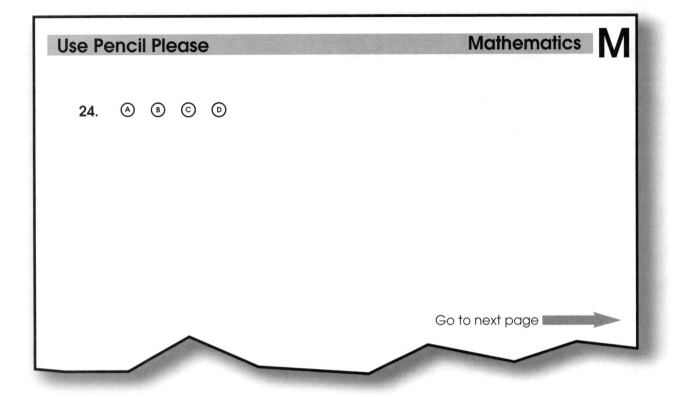

24. Ⓐ Ⓑ Ⓒ Ⓓ

Go to next page ▶

Analysis: *The correct answer is Choice A. A face of a three-dimensional solid is a flat polygon. This prism has two right triangular faces and three rectangular faces for a total of 5 faces. This eliminates all other choices. A vertex (plural: vertices) of a three-dimensional solid is a point where three or more faces meet. This prism has six vertices, three at each of the angles of the top triangle and three at each of the angles of the bottom triangle.*

Question **25** *assesses:*

Geometry and Spatial Sense Standard

Benchmark D: Identify, describe and classify types of line pairs, angles, two-dimensional figures and three-dimensional objects using their properties.

4. Identify and define relationships between planes; i.e., parallel, perpendicular and intersecting.

Mathematics **M**

25. Which of the following statements is true about this right triangular prism?

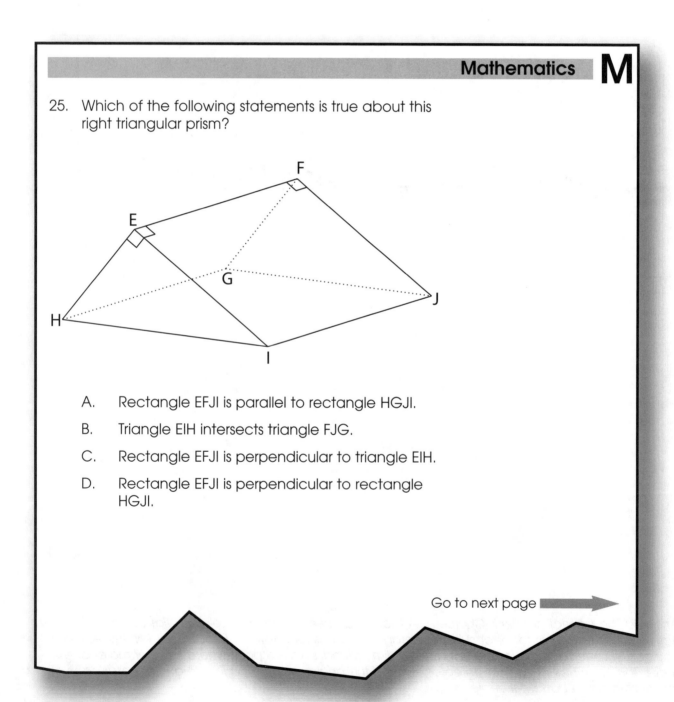

A. Rectangle EFJI is parallel to rectangle HGJI.

B. Triangle EIH intersects triangle FJG.

C. Rectangle EFJI is perpendicular to triangle EIH.

D. Rectangle EFJI is perpendicular to rectangle HGJI.

Go to next page ➡

Use Pencil Please · Mathematics M

25. Ⓐ Ⓑ Ⓒ Ⓓ

Go to next page ➤

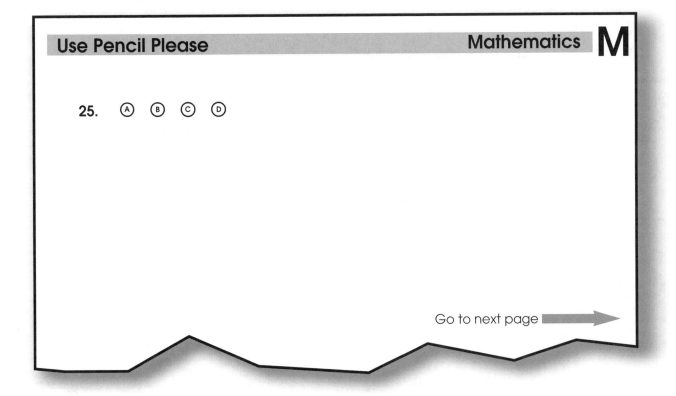

Analysis: *The correct answer is Choice C. Rectangle EFJI is perpendicular to triangle EIH as all the rectangles are perpendicular to both triangular bases. Choice A is incorrect because rectangle EFJI is not parallel to rectangle HGJI since they intersect at line JI. Choice B is incorrect because triangle EIH does not intersect triangle FJG; they are parallel. Choice D is incorrect because rectangle EFJI is not perpendicular to HGJI because angle EIH cannot be a right angle. Angle HEI is shown to be a right angle and a triangle cannot have two right angles.*

Question **26** *assesses:*

Geometry and Spatial Sense Standard

Benchmark F: Describe and use the concepts of congruence, similarity and symmetry to solve problems.

6. Draw similar figures that model proportional relationships; e.g., model similar figures with a 1 to 2 relationship by sketching two of the same figure, one with corresponding sides twice the length of the other.

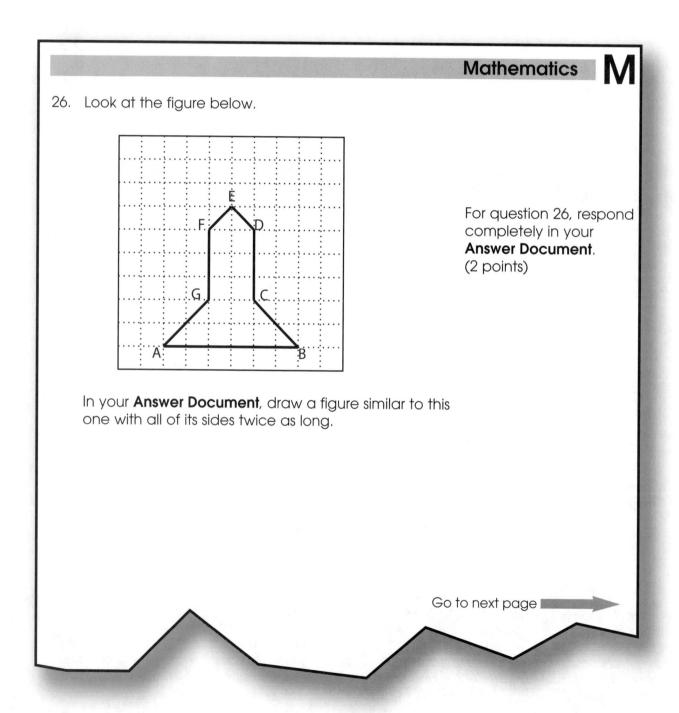

Mathematics M

26. Look at the figure below.

For question 26, respond completely in your **Answer Document**. (2 points)

In your **Answer Document**, draw a figure similar to this one with all of its sides twice as long.

Go to next page ➡

© Englefield & Associates, Inc.

Use Pencil Please

Mathematics M

26. Write your response to question 26 in the space below.

Go to next page ➡

Analysis: *In order to be similar, two figures must have the same shape, but not necessarily the same size. The easiest way to draw a shape twice as large is to start at the bottom and multiply everything by 2. For instance, the original shape's point A is one unit up and two units right of the bottom left corner. The enlarged shape should have Point A two units up and four units to the right of its bottom left corner. Line AB on the original figure is 6 units long, so line AB on the enlarged figure should be 12 units long. Line BC on the enlarged figure should go through the diagonals of four squares. Continue in this fashion until completed.*

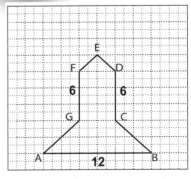

*Question **27** assesses:*

Geometry and Spatial Sense Standard

Benchmark G: Describe and use properties of triangles to solve problems involving angle measures and side lengths of right triangles.

3.   Use multiple classification criteria to classify triangles; e.g., right scalene triangle.

Mathematics M

27.   Look at the drawing below.

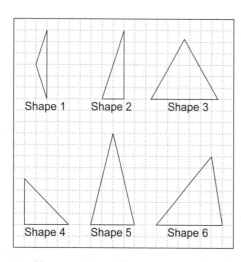

Which of the following statements is true about these triangles?

A.   There is at least one acute isosceles triangle, one right isosceles triangle, and one obtuse isosceles triangle in this set.

B.   There is at least one equilateral right triangle, one isosceles right triangle, and one scalene right triangle in this set.

C.   There is at least one acute scalene triangle, one right scalene triangle, and one obtuse scalene triangle in this set.

D.   There is at least one acute equilateral triangle, one right equilateral triangle, and one obtuse equilateral triangle in this set.

Go to next page ▶

Use Pencil Please

Mathematics **M**

27. Ⓐ Ⓑ Ⓒ Ⓓ

Go to next page ➡

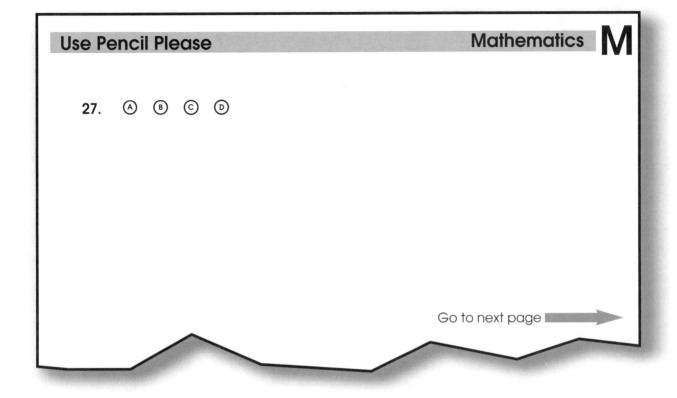

Shape 1   Shape 2   Shape 3

Shape 4   Shape 5   Shape 6

Analysis: *The correct answer is Choice A. An acute triangle has three angles that measure less than 90°, a right triangle has one angle that measures 90°, and an obtuse triangle has one angle that measures more than 90°. An equilateral triangle has three sides the same length, an isosceles triangle has at least two sides that measure the same length, and a scalene triangle has no sides that measure the same length. (Note that by this definition, an equilateral triangle is also an isosceles triangle.) Choice B is incorrect because there is no such thing as an equilateral right triangle. If a triangle is equilateral, it is also equiangular and all of its angles measure 60°. It would have no 90° angles. Choice C is incorrect because there is only one obtuse triangle in this set and it is an obtuse isosceles triangle. It is possible to have an obtuse scalene triangle, but none have been included here. Choice D is incorrect because there is no such thing as a right equilateral triangle or an obtuse equilateral triangle. If a triangle is equilateral, it is also equiangular and all of its angles measure 60°. It would have no 90° angles or angles greater than 90°.*

Shape	Angle Measure	Type of Triangle
1	obtuse	isoceles
2	right	scalene
3	acute/ equiangular	equilateral
4	right	isoceles
5	acute	isoceles
6	acute	scalene

Question **28** *assesses:*

Geometry and Spatial Sense Standard

Benchmark H: Predict and describe results (size, position, orientation) of transformations of two-dimensional figures.

5. Predict and describe sizes, positions and orientations of two-dimensional shapes after transformations such as reflections, rotations, translations and dilations.

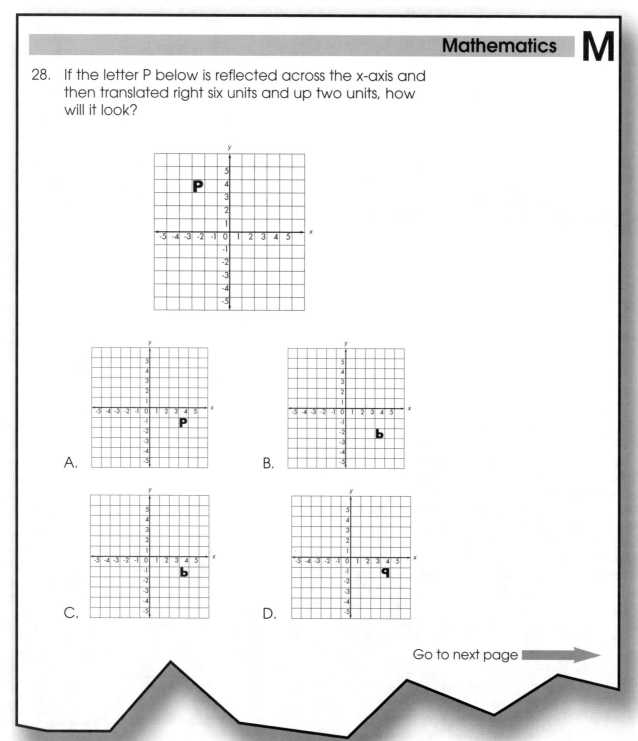

Mathematics **M**

28. If the letter P below is reflected across the x-axis and then translated right six units and up two units, how will it look?

A.

B.

C.

D.

Go to next page

Use Pencil Please

Mathematics M

28. (A) (B) (C) (D)

Go to next page ➡

Analysis: *The correct answer is Choice C. If the letter is reflected across the x-axis, it will be upside down the same number of units below the axis as it currently is above the axis. Choices A and D must be incorrect because neither is upside down. Since the letter starts in the third column left of the y-axis and the fourth row above the x-axis, when it's reflected across the x-axis it will still be in the third column left of the y-axis but now will be in the fourth row below the x-axis. Translating it six units right and two units up will put it in fourth column right of the y-axis and the second row below the x-axis. This is the location of Choice C. Choice B is incorrect because it is in the third row below the x-axis instead of the second.*

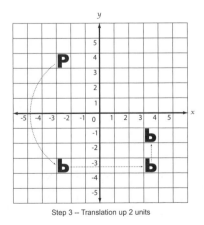

Step 3 -- Translation up 2 units

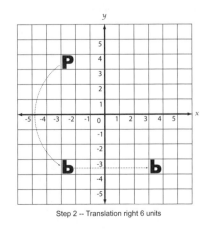

Step 2 -- Translation right 6 units

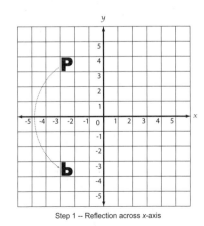

Step 1 -- Reflection across x-axis

Question **29** *assesses:*

Geometry and Spatial Sense Standard

Benchmark I: Identify and draw three-dimensional objects from different views (top, side, front and perspective).

7. Build three-dimensional objects with cubes, and sketch the two-dimensional representations of each side; i.e., projection sets.

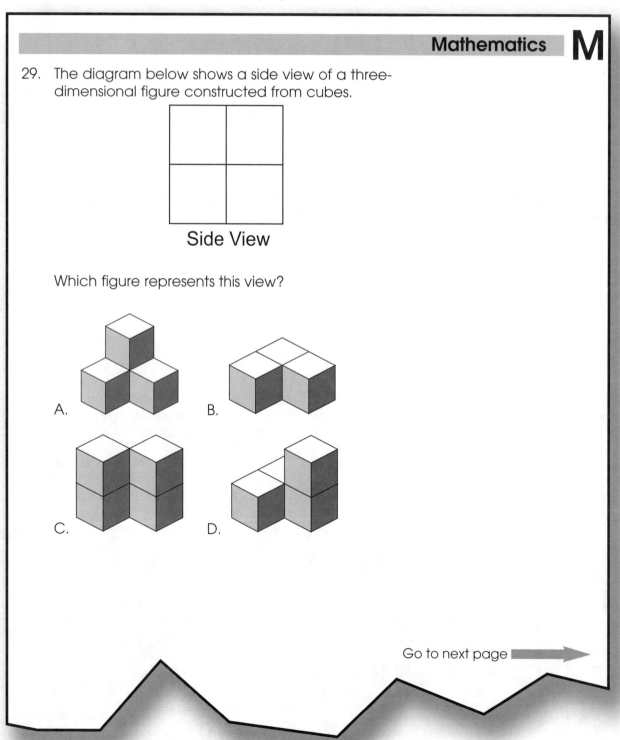

Mathematics **M**

29. The diagram below shows a side view of a three-dimensional figure constructed from cubes.

Side View

Which figure represents this view?

A.

B.

C.

D.

Go to next page ➡

© Englefield & Associates, Inc.

29. Ⓐ Ⓑ Ⓒ Ⓓ

Go to next page ➡

Analysis: *The correct answer is Choice C. If an observer stands perpendicular to any of the side faces, Choice C is the only shape that would look like the side view in the question. The other three choices would look like the diagrams at the right.*

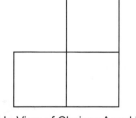

Side View of Choices A and D

Tutorial View of Choice B

Question **30** *assesses:*

Geometry and Spatial Sense Standard

Benchmark J: Apply properties of equality and proportionality to solve problems involving congruent or similar figures; e.g., create a scale drawing.

6. Draw similar figures that model proportional relationships; e.g., model similar figures with a 1 to 2 relationship by sketching two of the same figure, one with corresponding sides twice the length of the other.

Mathematics **M**

30. Tori drew the following sketch of a wooden deck she wants to add to her house. She intends to use this drawing to plan how she will arrange her outdoor furniture and barbeque when the deck is finished. She is satisfied with the deck's shape, but is worried that the drawing is too small for her purpose.

For question 30, respond completely in your **Answer Document**. (2 points)

Deck Plan

In your **Answer Document**, draw a larger outline of the deck with sides in a ratio of 3 to 1 to the original drawing.

Go to next page ➡

Copying is Prohibited

Use Pencil Please

Mathematics M

30. Write your response to question 30 in the space below.

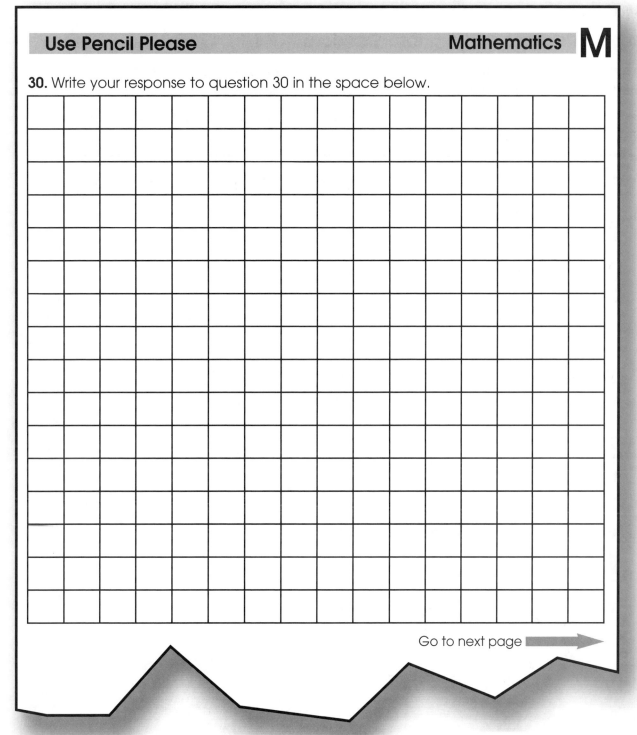

Go to next page ➡

Analysis: *The easiest way to enlarge the scale of this drawing as the question requires is to multiply all of the lengths by 3. Starting at the bottom, since line AB on the original drawing is 5 units long, make line AB on the enlarged drawing 15 units. Line BC on the original drawing is 2 units long, so line BC on the enlarged drawing must be 6 units. Line CD on the original drawing goes through the diagonal of one square, so line CK on the enlarged drawing should go through the diagonals of three squares. Line DE on the original is 3 units long, so line DE on the enlarged drawing must be nine units long. Continue in this fashion until the enlargement is complete.*

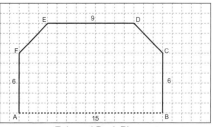

Enlarged Deck Plan

Question **31** *assesses:*

Patterns, Functions and Algebra Standard

Benchmark A: Describe, extend and determine the rule for patterns and relationships occurring in numeric patterns, computation, geometry, graphs and other applications.

1. Represent and analyze patterns, rules and functions, using physical materials, tables and graphs.

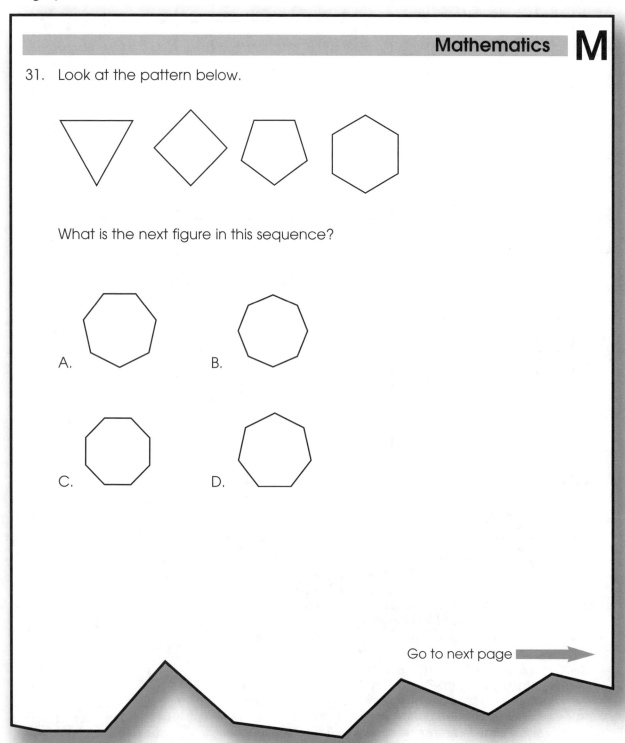

Mathematics M

31. Look at the pattern below.

What is the next figure in this sequence?

A.

B.

C.

D.

Go to next page ➡

Copying is Prohibited   © Englefield & Associates, Inc.

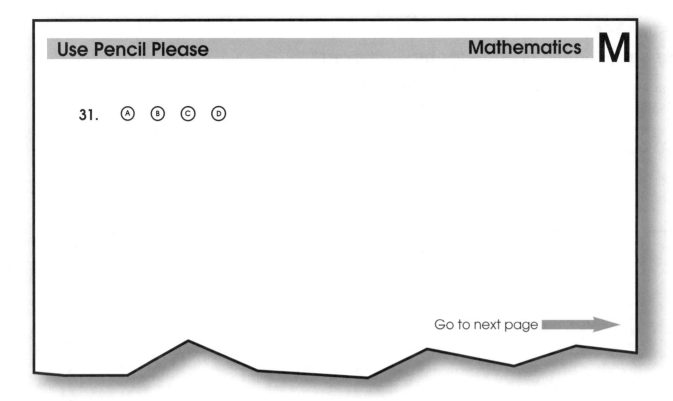

Use Pencil Please

Mathematics **M**

31. Ⓐ Ⓑ Ⓒ Ⓓ

Go to next page ➡

Analysis: The correct answer is Choice A. The pattern here is 3 sides, 4 sides, 5 sides, and 6 sides balanced on one vertex at the bottom of the figure. The next figure then should be 7 sides balanced on a vertex at the bottom, Choice A. Choice B is incorrect because it has 8 sides. Choice C is incorrect because it has eight sides and is not balanced on a vertex. Choice D is incorrect because it is not balanced on a vertex.

Question **32** *assesses:*

Patterns, Functions and Algebra Standard

Benchmark A: Describe, extend and determine the rule for patterns and relationships occurring in numeric patterns, computation, geometry, graphs and other applications.

2. Use words and symbols to describe numerical and geometric patterns, rules and functions.

Mathematics **M**

32. John created the number pattern shown.

5, 30, 155, 780, 3905, ...

Which rule describes how to find the next term in John's pattern?

A. Multiply the previous number by five and add five.

B. Multiply the previous number by six.

C. Multiply the previous two numbers together and add five.

D. Multiply the previous number by ten and subtract 20.

Go to next page ➡

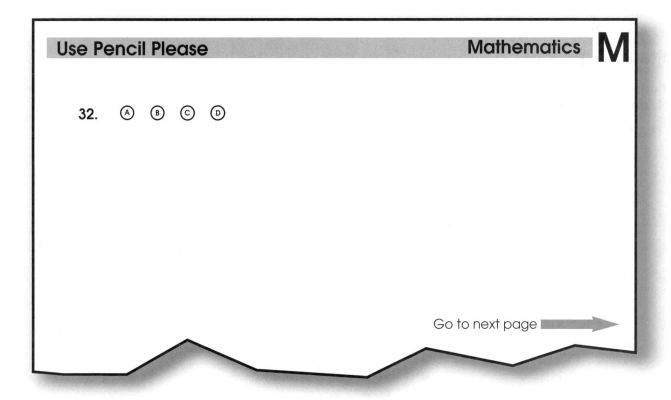

Use Pencil Please

Mathematics M

32. Ⓐ Ⓑ Ⓒ Ⓓ

Go to next page ➡

Analysis: The correct answer is Choice A (5 x 5 + 5 = 25 + 5 = 30; 5 x 30 + 5 = 150 + 5 = 155; 5 x 155 + 5 = 775 + 5 = 780; 5 x 780 + 5 = 3900 + 5 = 3905). Choice B is incorrect because it only produces the second term in the number pattern. The correct rule must produce all of the terms in the number pattern. Choice C is incorrect because it only produces the third term in the number pattern. The correct rule must produce all of the terms in the number pattern. Choice D is incorrect because it only produces the second term in the number pattern. The correct rule must produce all of the terms in the number pattern.

Question **33** *assesses:*

Patterns, Functions and Algebra Standard

Benchmark C: Use variables to create and solve equations and inequalities representing problem situations.

5. Produce and interpret graphs that represent the relationship between two variables.

Mathematics **M**

33. Ms. Gardner's class conducted an experiment in science class to see how long it would take various kinds of vegetable seeds to germinate under identical conditions. They planted five seeds of each type, recorded when each seed sprouted, and calculated the average germination time of each plant variety. Their results were as follows:

For question 33, respond completely in your **Answer Document**. (4 points)

Plant	Average Germination Time
carrots	12 days
radishes	8 days
lettuce	10 days
onions	6 days
asparagus	21 days
sweet corn	8 days
pumpkins	8 days

In your **Answer Document**, construct a bar graph to display this data.

Go to next page

Use Pencil Please   Mathematics M

33. Write your response to question 33 in the space below.

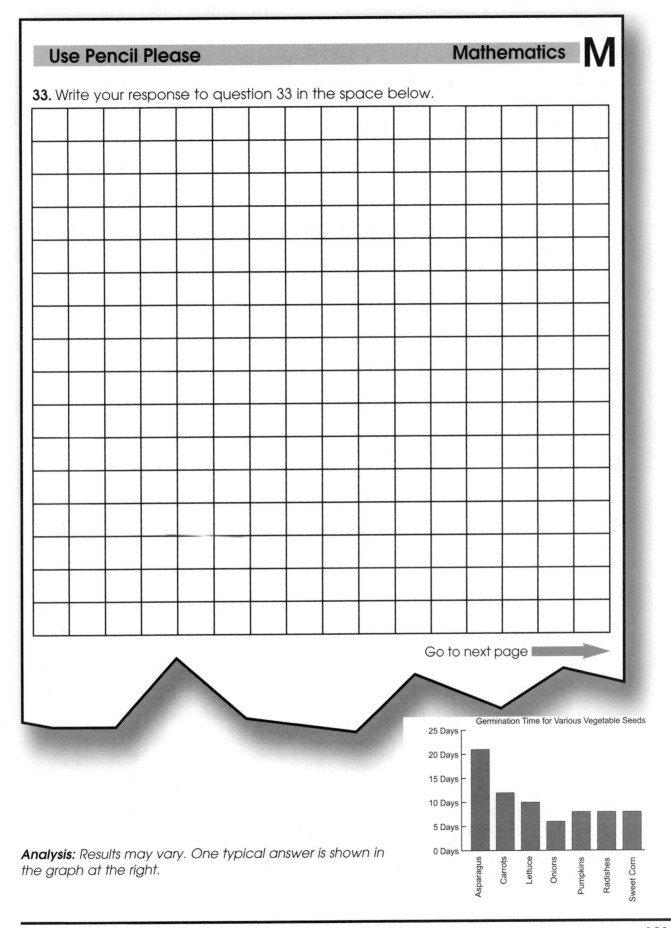

Go to next page ➤

Germination Time for Various Vegetable Seeds

Analysis: *Results may vary. One typical answer is shown in the graph at the right.*

Question **34** *assesses:*

Patterns, Functions and Algebra Standard

Benchmark C: Use variables to create and solve equations and inequalities representing problem situations.

6. Evaluate simple expressions by replacing variables with given values, and use formulas in problem-solving situations.

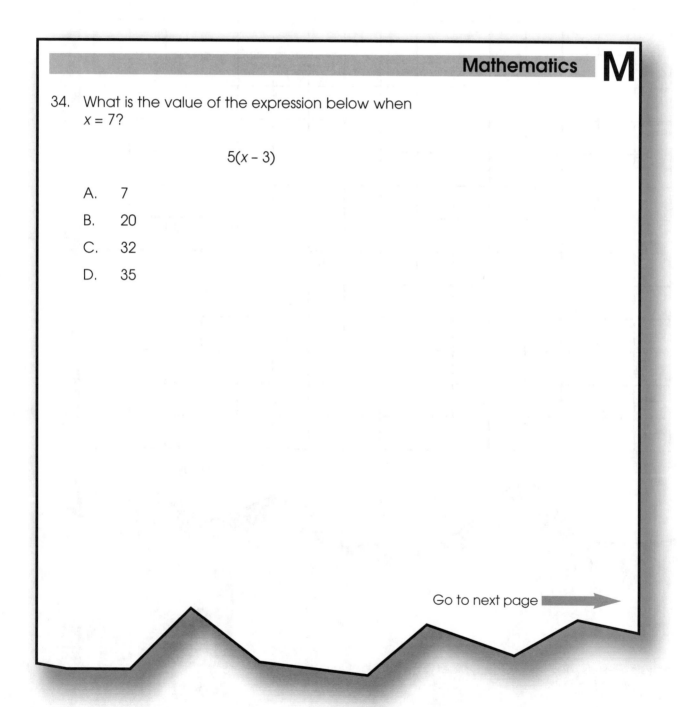

Mathematics **M**

34. What is the value of the expression below when $x = 7$?

$$5(x - 3)$$

    A.   7

    B.   20

    C.   32

    D.   35

Go to next page ➡

Use Pencil Please

Mathematics **M**

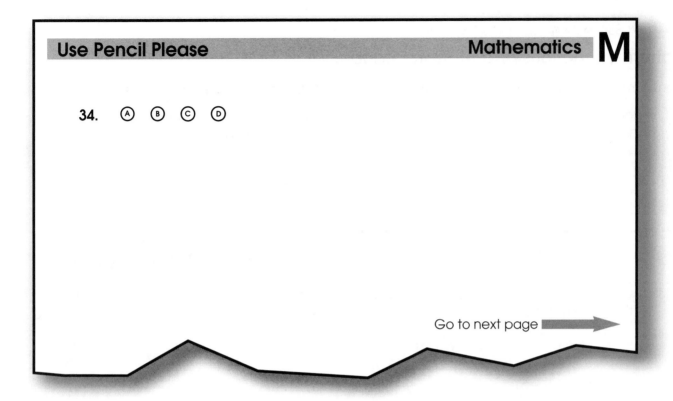

34. Ⓐ Ⓑ Ⓒ Ⓓ

Go to next page ▶

Analysis: *The correct answer is Choice B; 5(x – 3) = 5(7 – 3) = 5(4) = 20. Choice A is incorrect because 7 is only the value of x, not the value of the entire expression when x = 7. Choice C is incorrect because 32 is the answer you get when you multiply 5 times 7 and then subtract 3, instead of subtracting 3 from 7 first and then multiplying by 5. Choice D is incorrect because the – 3 is left out of the solution entirely. The 7 is substituted in for x and then multiplied by 5 while the – 3 is ignored.*

Question **35** *assesses:*

Patterns, Functions and Algebra Standard

Benchmark D: Use symbolic algebra to represent and explain mathematical relationships.

3. Recognize and generate equivalent forms of algebraic expressions, and explain how the commutative, associative and distributive properties can be used to generate equivalent forms; e.g., perimeter as $2(l + w)$ or $2l + 2w$.

Mathematics **M**

35. Which expression does not have the same value as the expression below?

$$3 - 7(8 - 5) + 21$$

A. $24 - 7(8 - 5)$

B. $3 - 7(3) + 21$

C. $3 - 56 + 35 + 21$

D. $-7(8 - 5) + 18$

Go to next page ▶

Copying is Prohibited   © Englefield & Associates, Inc.

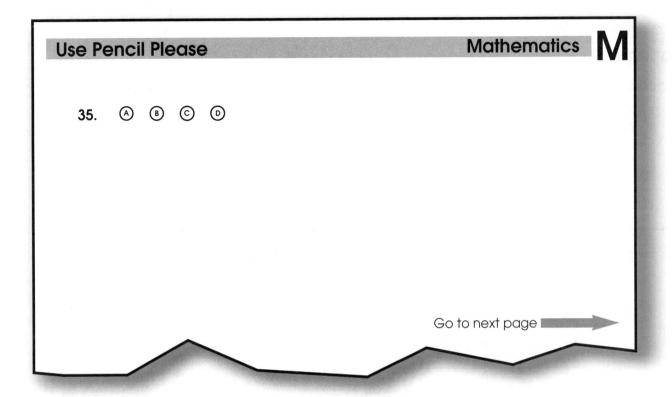

Use Pencil Please　　　　　　　　　　**Mathematics** M

35.　Ⓐ　Ⓑ　Ⓒ　Ⓓ

Go to next page ➡

Analysis: *The correct answer is Choice D. Using the correct order of operations, the expression simplifies to 3; 3 – 7(8 – 5) + 21; 3 – 7(3) + 21; 3 – 21 + 21; 24 – 21 = 3. Choice A is incorrect because it can be simplified to 3: 24 – 7(8 – 5); 24 – 7(3); 24 – 21 = 3. Choice B is incorrect because it can be simplified to 3: 3 – 7(3) + 21; 3 – 21 + 21 = 3. Choice C is incorrect because it can be simplified to 3: 3 – 56 + 35 + 21; 3 + 35 + 21 – 56; 59 – 56 = 3. Choice D is correct because in does not simplify to 3: – 7(8 – 5) + 18; –7(3) + 18, –21 + 18 = –3.*

Question **36** *assesses:*

Patterns, Functions and Algebra Standard

Benchmark E: Use rules and variables to describe patterns, functions and other relationships.

2. Use words and symbols to describe numerical and geometric patterns, rules and functions.

Mathematics

36. What is the rule to find the term value in the number pattern below?

Term Number, n	Term Value
1	4
2	7
3	10
4	13
5	16
n	?

A. The term number plus three.

B. Two times the term number plus two.

C. Three times the term number plus one.

D. Four times the term number minus one.

Go to next page ➡

Copying is Prohibited   © Englefield & Associates, Inc.

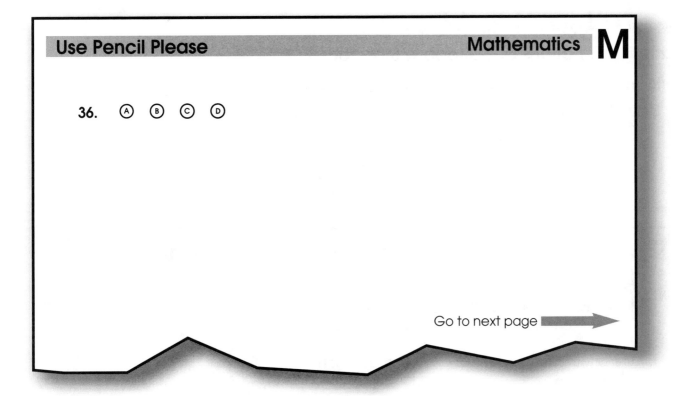

Use Pencil Please

Mathematics **M**

36. Ⓐ Ⓑ Ⓒ Ⓓ

Go to next page ➤

Analysis: *The correct answer is Choice C. In order to be correct, the rule must be true for every term in the number pattern and this one is: 3(1) + 1 = 4; 3(2) + 1 = 7; 3(3) + 1 = 10; 3(4) + 1 = 13; 3(5) + 1 = 16; Choice A is incorrect because it only works for the first term in the number pattern and it must work for all terms in the number pattern. Choice B is incorrect because it only works for the first term in the number pattern and it must work for all terms in the number pattern. Choice D is incorrect because it only works for the second term in the number pattern and it must work for all terms in the number pattern.*

Question **37** *assesses:*

Patterns, Functions and Algebra Standard

Benchmark G: Write, simplify and evaluate algebraic expressions.

6. Evaluate simple expressions by replacing variables with given values, and use formulas in problem-solving situations.

Mathematics

37. The Union Pacific Big Boy was the largest steam locomotive ever built. The locomotive had 24 wheels, 16 of which were 68-inch drive wheels.

    If a drive wheel from this locomotive is 68 inches in diameter, what is its circumference? ($C = 2\pi r$ or $C = \pi d$.)

    A.   approximately 68 inches or about $5\frac{1}{2}$ feet

    B.   approximately 107 inches or about 9 feet

    C.   approximately 214 inches or about 18 feet

    D.   approximately 427 inches or about $35\frac{1}{2}$ feet

Go to next page ➡

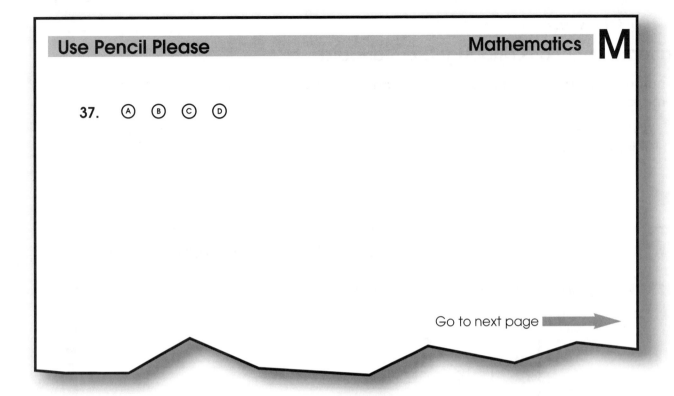

Use Pencil Please
                 Mathematics **M**

37. Ⓐ   Ⓑ   Ⓒ   Ⓓ

Go to next page ➡

Analysis: The correct answer is Choice C. The diameter is given as 68 inches so this can be substituted into the second given formula for circumference using 3.14 as a value for pi: $C = \pi d$; $C \approx 3.14 \times 68 \approx 213.52 \approx 214$ inches ≈ 18 feet. Choice A is incorrect because this is just the diameter of the wheel, not the circumference. This is how tall the wheel would be if you stood next to it. Choice B is incorrect because this answer comes from taking half the diameter to find the radius, but then substituting it into the second formula instead of the first. Choice D is incorrect because this answer treats the given diameter like a radius and substitutes it into the first formula instead of the second.

Question **38** *assesses:*

Patterns, Functions and Algebra Standard

Benchmark H: Solve linear equations and inequalities symbolically, graphically and numerically.

4. Solve simple linear equations and inequalities using physical models, paper and pencil, tables and graphs.

Mathematics **M**

38. An equation and its graph are given below.

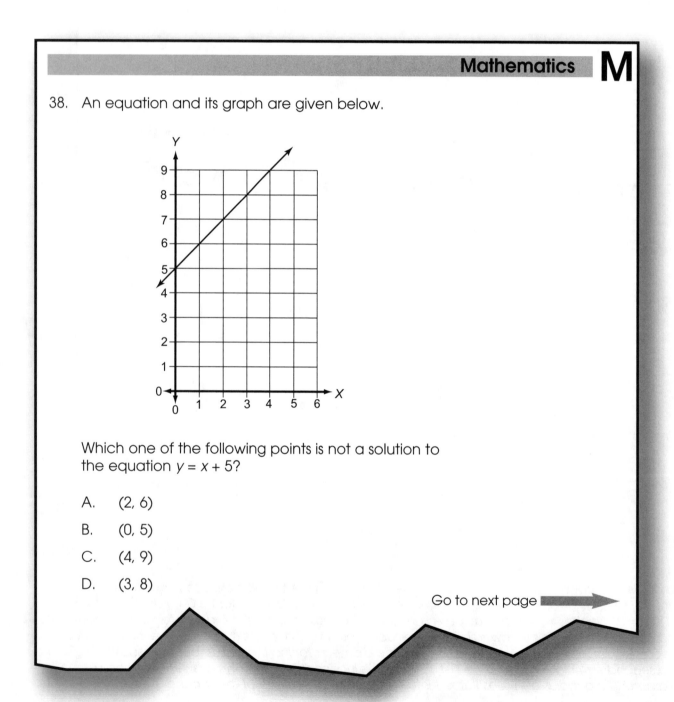

Which one of the following points is not a solution to the equation $y = x + 5$?

A. (2, 6)

B. (0, 5)

C. (4, 9)

D. (3, 8)

Go to next page ➡

Copying is Prohibited © Englefield & Associates, Inc.

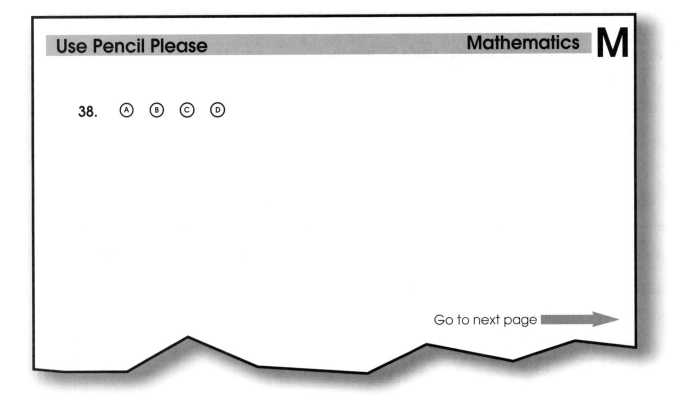

Use Pencil Please

Mathematics **M**

38. Ⓐ   Ⓑ   Ⓒ   Ⓓ

Go to next page ▶

Analysis: *The correct answer is Choice A. There are two ways to check if a point is a solution to an equation. First, it must appear on the graph of the equation. If you look at point (2, 6) on the grid, you will see that it is not on the graph of this line, so (2,6) cannot be a solution of y = x + 5. Second, if the x-coordinate is substituted for x and the y-coordinate is substituted for y in the equation, a true mathematical sentence will result. In this case: y = x + 5; 6 = 2 + 5. Since this statement is false, (2, 6) cannot be a solution of y = x + 5. Since we are to find the point that is not a solution, Choice A is correct. Choice B is incorrect because (0, 5) is on the graph of the line and y = x + 5; 5 = 0 + 5 is a true mathematical sentence. Choice C is incorrect because (4, 9) is on the graph of the line and y = x + 5; 9 = 4 + 5 is a true mathematical sentence. Choice D is incorrect because (3, 8) is on the graph of the line and y = x + 5; 8 = 3 + 5 is a true mathematical sentence.*

Question **39** *assesses:*

Patterns, Functions and Algebra Standard

Benchmark J: Use formulas in problem-solving situations.

2. Use words and symbols to describe numerical and geometric patterns, rules and functions.

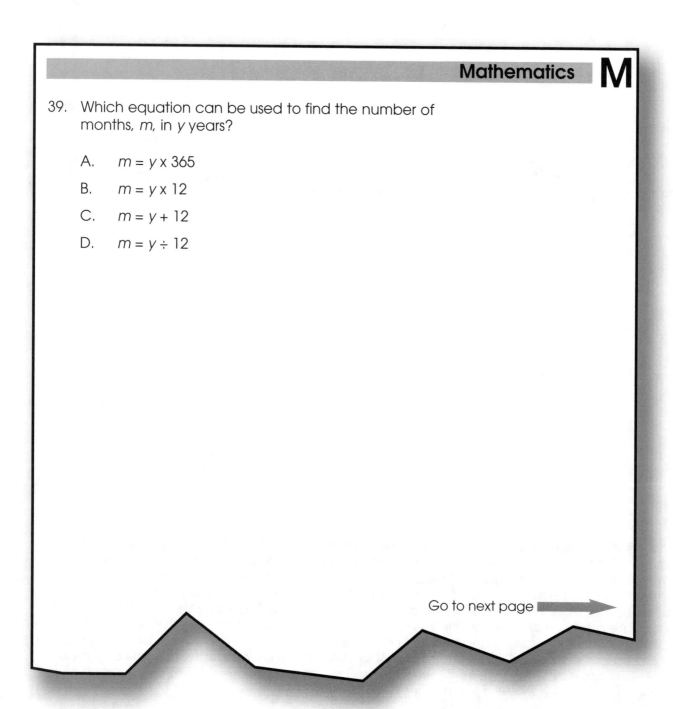

Mathematics M

39. Which equation can be used to find the number of months, *m*, in *y* years?

   A. $m = y \times 365$

   B. $m = y \times 12$

   C. $m = y + 12$

   D. $m = y \div 12$

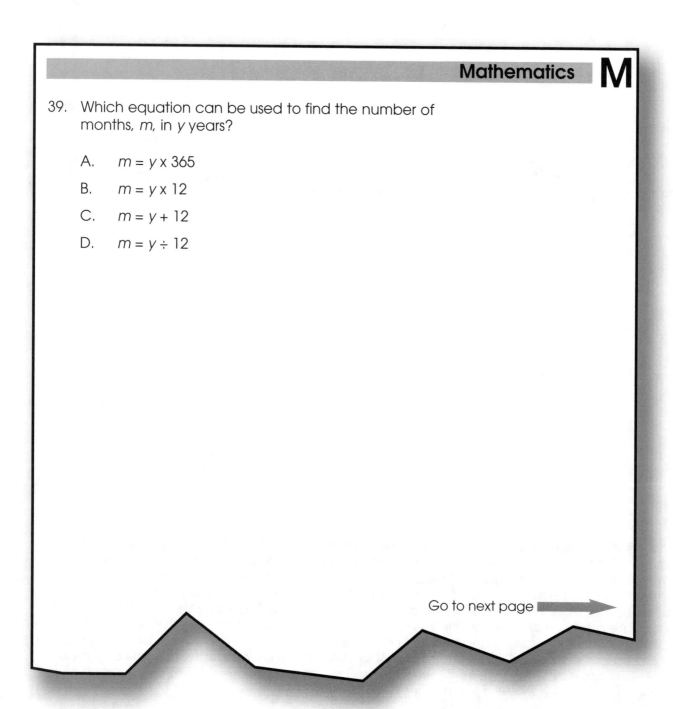

Go to next page ➡

© Englefield & Associates, Inc.

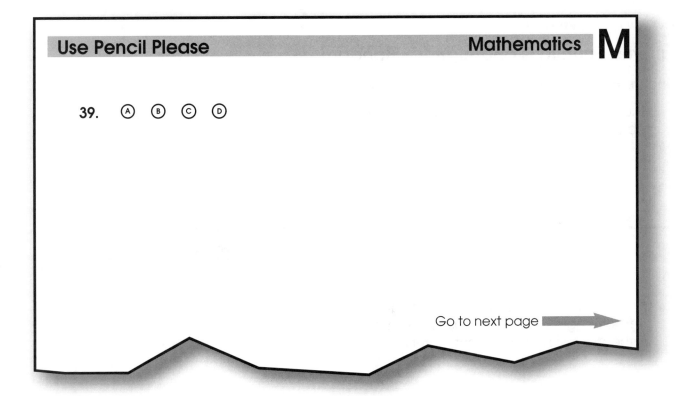

Use Pencil Please   **Mathematics** M

39. Ⓐ Ⓑ Ⓒ Ⓓ

Go to next page ➡

Analysis: The correct answer is Choice B. Since there are 12 months in each year, you must multiply the number of years, y, by 12 to find the number of months, m. Choice A is incorrect because multiplying y by 365 will give the number of days in y years, not the number of months. Choice C is incorrect because you need to multiply y times 12, not add y to 12. Choice C is incorrect because you need to multiply y times 12, not divide y by 12. This answer will give a number of months that is smaller than the number of years.

Question **40** *assesses:*

Patterns, Functions and Algebra Standard

Benchmark J: Use formulas in problem-solving situations.

6. Evaluate simple expressions by replacing variables with given values, and use formulas in problem-solving situations.

Mathematics **M**

40. The formula for the area of a triangle is $A = \frac{1}{2}bh$. In the triangle below, the base is 4 cm and the area is 22 square centimeters.

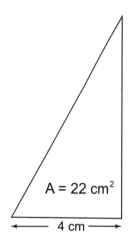

$A = 22 \text{ cm}^2$

← 4 cm →

What is the height of this triangle?

A.   11 cm

B.   11 cm²

C.   22 cm

D.   44 cm

Go to next page ➡

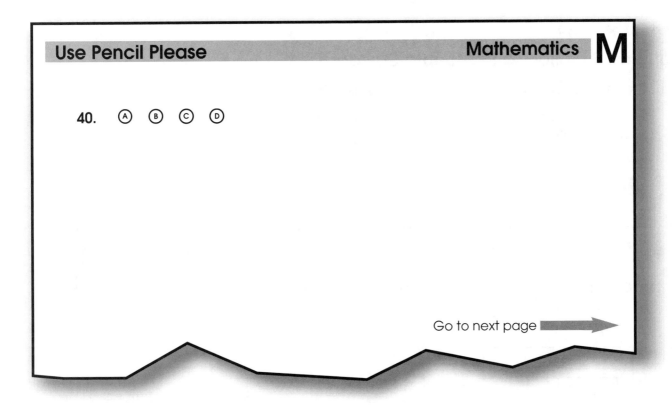

Use Pencil Please

Mathematics M

40. Ⓐ Ⓑ Ⓒ Ⓓ

Go to next page ➡

Analysis: The correct answer is Choice A. First, replace the variables in the formula with the numbers you are given, then simplify: $A = \frac{1}{2}bh$; $22 = \frac{1}{2}(4)h$; $22 = 2h$ (since $\frac{1}{2}(4) = 2$); $h = 11$ cm. Choice B is incorrect because height is measured in linear units, not square units, which are used to measure area. Choice C is incorrect because 22 is the area of the triangle, not the height. Choice D is incorrect because both sides of the equation are multiplied by 2 instead of being divided by two at this step: $22 = 2h$.

Question **41** *assesses:*

Patterns, Functions and Algebra Standard

Benchmark K: Graph linear equations and inequalities.

4. Solve simple linear equations and inequalities using physical models, paper and pencil, tables and graphs.

Mathematics **M**

41. Calculate the correct *y* value for each *x* value in the table below.

$y = 2x - 1$	
x	*y*
1	
2	
3	
4	

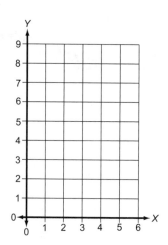

For question 41, respond completely in your **Answer Document**. (2 points)

Use the coordinates to construct a graph of the equation in your **Answer Document**.

Go to next page ▬▬▶

Copying is Prohibited

© Englefield & Associates, Inc.

41. Write your response to question 41 in the space below.

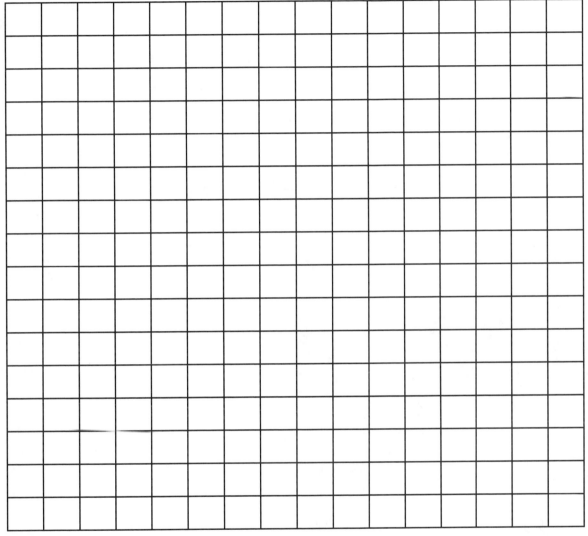

Go to next page ➡

Analysis: *Substitute each value of x into the equation*
y = 2x – 1 and calculate y.

If x = 1, then y = 2(1) – 1; y = 2 – 1; y = 1
If x = 2, then y = 2(2) – 1; y = 4 – 1; y = 3
If x = 3, then y = 2(3) – 1; y = 6 – 1; y = 5
If x = 4, then y = 2(4) – 1; y = 8 – 1; y = 7

Now you have an x-value and a y-value for four points:
(1, 1), (2, 3), (3, 5), and (4, 7). Plot these points on the grid
and connect them with a straight line.

$y = 2x - 1$	
x	y
1	1
2	3
3	5
4	7

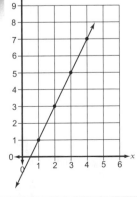

Question **42** *assesses:*

Patterns, Functions and Algebra Standard

Benchmark K: Graph linear equations and inequalities.

5. Produce and interpret graphs that represent the relationship between two variables.

Mathematics **M**

42. The graph below shows the number of named tropical storms in the Atlantic Ocean each year from 1997 to 2005.

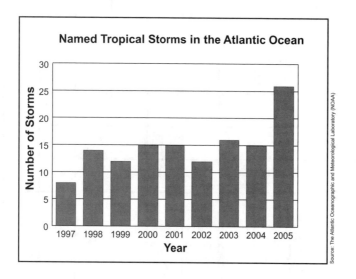

Named Tropical Storms in the Atlantic Ocean

Source: The Atlantic Oceanographic and Meteorological Laboratory (NOAA)

Which statement can be supported with data from the graph?

A.   2005 had the most tropical storms in history.

B.   Pollution is causing an increase in tropical storms.

C.   Every year during this period has seen an increase in the number of tropical storms in the Atlantic Ocean.

D.   During this nine-year period, it seems that number of tropical storms may be increasing in the Atlantic Ocean.

Go to next page ➡

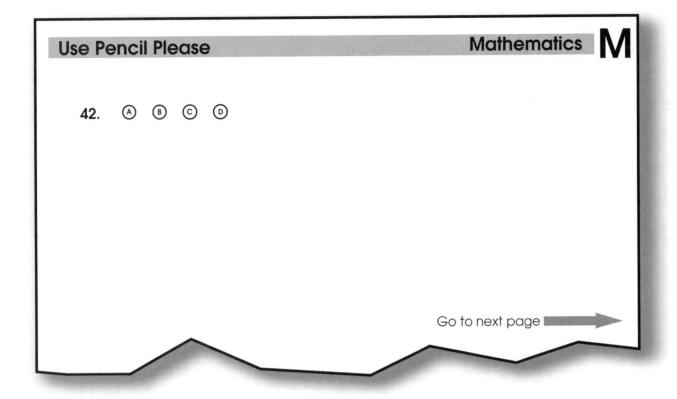

Use Pencil Please

Mathematics M

42. Ⓐ Ⓑ Ⓒ Ⓓ

Go to next page ➤

Analysis: *The correct answer is Choice D. During the nine-year period covered by this graph, there seems to be increasing tropical storm activity. Data does not have to show a straight line to reveal a trend. In this case, some years the level of storm activity is up and sometimes it is down. However, over this short time period, the number of storms seems to be gradually rising. Choice A is incorrect because the graph only shows nine years of record keeping. The year 2005 has the highest level of tropical storm activity during this time period, but there may have been some higher level of activity in a previous year that was not included in this data. In other words, Choice A may be true, but it cannot be supported with data from this graph. Choice B is incorrect because the data in the graph only shows how many storms occurred in each year. It says nothing about the cause of these storms. Again, Choice B may be true, but it cannot be supported with data from this graph. Choice C is incorrect because it is clearly false. It is easy to see, for instance, that 1999 had fewer tropical storms than 1998. In order for Choice C to be true, every year in the period must show an increase in storm activity from the previous year.*

Question **43** *assesses:*

Patterns, Functions and Algebra Standard

Benchmark L: Analyze functional relationships, and explain how a change in one quantity results in a change in the other.

7. Identify and describe situations with constant or varying rates of change, and compare them.

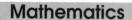 **Mathematics** M

43. On a short vacation together, Charlie and Martha kept track of how many miles they drove and how many gallons of gasoline they used. The graph below shows this data.

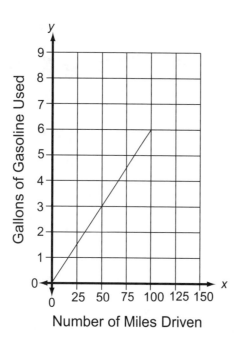

Number of Miles Driven

If they continue using gasoline at the same rate, how many gallons will they use on a trip of 125 miles?

A. 9 gallons

B. 8 gallons

C. between 7 and 8 gallons

D. less than 7 gallons

Go to next page ▶

Copying is Prohibited
© Englefield & Associates, Inc.

Use Pencil Please

Mathematics **M**

43.   Ⓐ   Ⓑ   Ⓒ   Ⓓ

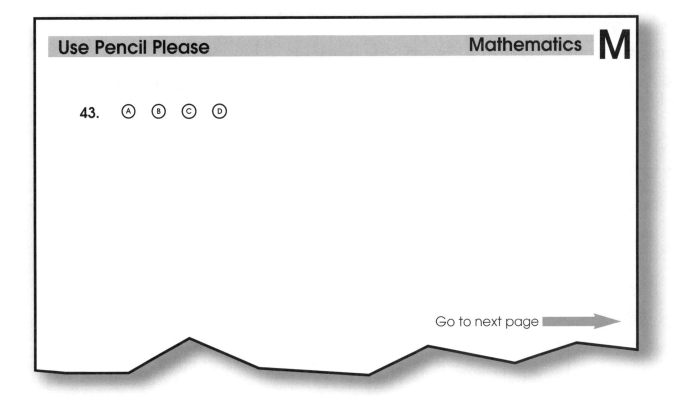

Go to next page ▶

Analysis: *The correct answer is Choice C. The question tells us to assume that the car continues to use gasoline at the same rate as on an earlier trip. This means that a graph of gasoline use on a new trip should follow this same straight line. The easiest way to solve this problem is to extend the straight line on the graph to see where it will intersect with the vertical line of 125 miles. In this case, it is between the 7 and the 8. Choice A is incorrect because this would be the gasoline used on a trip of 150 miles, not a trip of 125 miles. Choice B is incorrect because it is clear the graph of gasoline usage will not reach the 8 gallon horizontal line until some time after 125 miles. Choice D is incorrect because it is clear the graph of gasoline usage will reach the 7 gallon horizontal line before 125 miles is driven.*

Question **44** *assesses:*

Patterns, Functions and Algebra Standard

Benchmark M: Approximate and interpret rates of change from graphical and numerical data.

8. Use technology to analyze change; e.g., use computer applications or graphing calculators to display and interpret rate of change.

Mathematics **M**

44. During an experiment in science class, students fired a toy cannon and collected the following data about the height of the cannonball above the ground. They organized the data into the graph below.

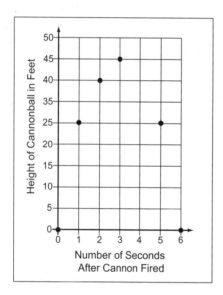

Unfortunately, Chuck, the class secretary, forgot to record the cannonball's height four seconds after the firing. What is the most likely height of the cannonball after four seconds?

A.   50 feet

B.   45 feet

C.   40 feet

D.   35 feet

Go to next page ➡

Use Pencil Please　　　　　　　　　　　　　　**Mathematics** M

44.　　Ⓐ　Ⓑ　Ⓒ　Ⓓ

Go to next page ➡

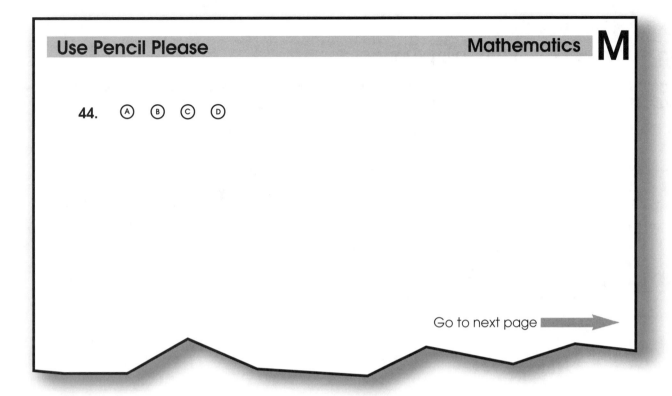

Analysis: *The correct answer is Choice C. A cannonball rises for a time until it reaches its maximum height and then falls back down to the ground. The curve that it traces on its flight through the sky is called a parabola. Parabolas are symmetrical around a vertical line or axis. Each point in the parabola (with the exception of the maximum point), has a mirror image point at the same height on the other side of the axis. For example, the cannonball is at the same height after 5 seconds as it was after 1 second—25 feet. Similarly, the cannonball is at the same height after 4 seconds as it was after 2 seconds—40 feet. The other choices are incorrect because putting a point at any of these heights after 4 seconds would ruin the symmetry of the curve.*

Question **45** *assesses:*

Data Analysis and Probability Standard

Benchmark A: Read, create and use line graphs, histograms, circle graphs, box-and-whisker plots, stem-and-leaf plots, and other representations when appropriate.

1. Read, construct and interpret line graphs, circle graphs and histograms.

Mathematics **M**

45. Maizy conducted a survey of the students in her class to find out what kind of snack food they preferred while attending a movie theatre. Of the students in the class, 63% said they preferred popcorn, 25% preferred candy, and 12% preferred chewing gum.

    Which graph best represents these data?

    A.

    Candy
    Popcorn
    Gum

    B.

    Candy
    Gum
    Popcorn

    C.

    Candy
    Popcorn
    Gum

    D.

    Candy
    Gum
    Popcorn

Go to next page ➡

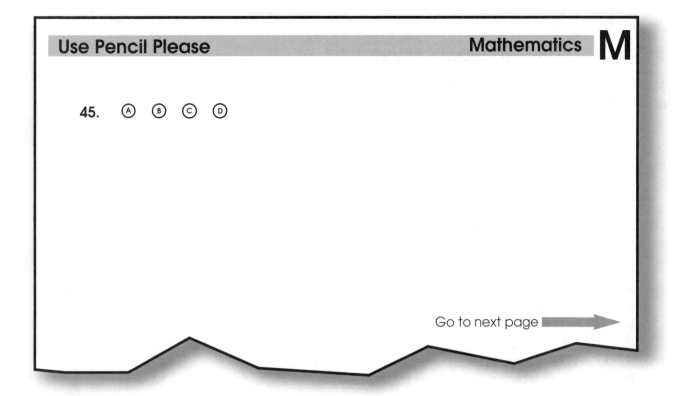

Analysis: The correct answer is Choice B. To answer this question, you must know how to estimate the fractional equivalents of percentages and be able to recognize the shape of a given fraction of a circle. Since $\frac{1}{2}$ = 50% and 63% of Maizy's classmates prefer popcorn, the part of the graph representing popcorn must be greater than half. This eliminates all of the choices except Choice B because they all show popcorn with a fraction of $\frac{1}{2}$ or less. In addition, since $\frac{1}{4}$ = 25%, candy should be shown as a quarter of the circle. Only Choices A and B do this. Choices C and D show candy as a fraction about equal to $\frac{1}{3}$. Because gum is favored by 12% of the class, it should be shown as about half the size of candy. Choice B is the only choice to show candy correctly.

Question **46** *assesses:*

Data Analysis and Probability Standard

Benchmark B: Interpret data by looking for patterns and relationships, draw and justify conclusions, and answer related questions.

5. Describe the frequency distribution of a set of data, as shown in a histogram or frequency table, by general appearance or shape; e.g., number of modes, middle of data, level of symmetry, outliers.

Mathematics **M**

46. In 1903, the Binney & Smith Company introduced the first box of Crayola® crayons. There were eight colors in the box. Rhonda decided to conduct a survey of all the sixth graders in her school to find which one of these colors each student preferred. The results of her study are summarized in the table below.

Favorite Color	Number of Students
black	16
blue	25
brown	3
green	16
orange	12
red	20
violet	17
yellow	15

Source: www.crayola.com

Which statement is true?

A.   There are two modes in this data set.

B.   The range of this data set is twelve.

C.   Violet is an outlier in this data set.

D.   The mode of this data set is sixteen.

Go to next page ➡

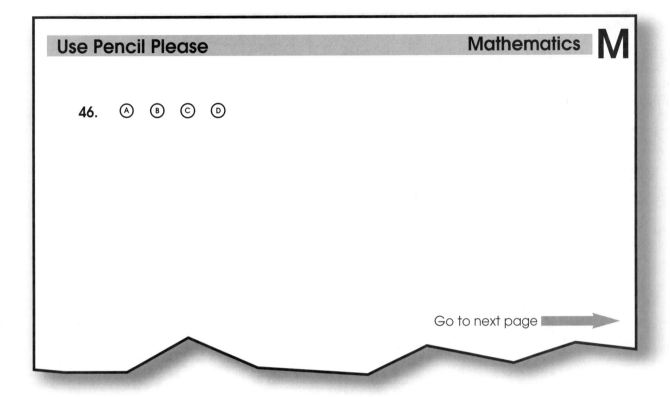

Analysis: The correct answer is Choice D. The mode of a set of data is the value or values that occur most often. In this data set, 16 occurs twice and all the other values occur only once, so 16 is the only mode. Choice A is incorrect since this data set has only one mode, 16. Choice B is incorrect because the range of a data set is the difference between its highest value and its lowest value. In this set, the range is 22 (25 – 3 = 22). Choice C is incorrect because an outlier is a value in the data set that is either very much lower or very much higher than the other values in the set. Since violet has 17 votes and 17 is in the middle of the set, it is not an outlier.

Question **47** *assesses:*

Data Analysis and Probability Standard

Benchmark D: Compare increasingly complex displays of data, such as multiple sets of data on the same graph.

3. Compare representations of the same data in different types of graphs, such as a bar graph and circle graph.

Mathematics **M**

47. The table below lists the six largest countries in the world in terms of area.

Largest Countries in Square Miles, 2004

1	Russia	6,592,735
2	Canada	3,855,081
3	United States	3,717,792
4	China	3,705,386
5	Brazil	3,286,470
6	Australia	2,967,893

Source: www.infoplease.com

Which graph best represents the data in the table?

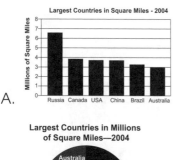

A.

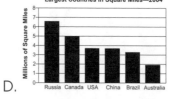

B.

C.

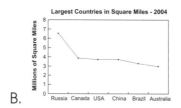

D.

Go to next page ▶

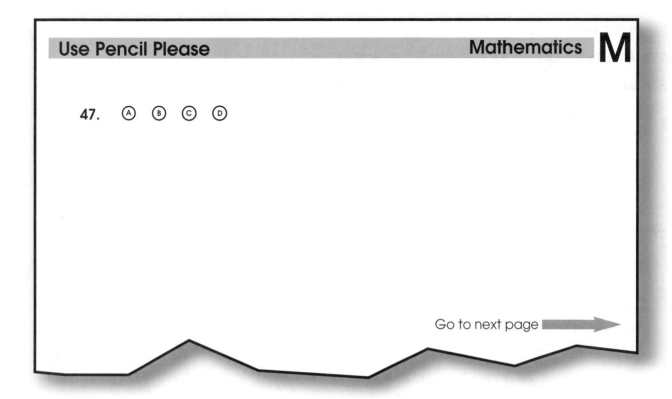

Use Pencil Please

Mathematics **M**

47. Ⓐ Ⓑ Ⓒ Ⓓ

Go to next page ➡

Analysis: *The correct answer is Choice A. Bar graphs like choices A or D are the best ways to display the data in this chart because they are very good for comparing things or showing ranked items. Choice B is incorrect because line graphs are usually used to show changes over time and this data is not about change. Choice C is incorrect because pie charts or circle graphs are used to show fractions of a whole. This data is not concerned with all the land in the world, only that occupied by the six largest countries. Choice D is incorrect because some of the data is displayed incorrectly. Canada is shown as having an area of 5 million square miles when its actual area is about 3.9 million square miles. Australia is shown as having an area of not quite 2 million square miles when its actual area is about 3 million square miles.*

Question **48** *assesses:*

Data Analysis and Probability Standard

Benchmark E: Collect, organize, display and interpret data for a specific purpose or need.

2. Select, create and use graphical representations that are appropriate for the type of data collected.

Mathematics **M**

48. If you wanted to keep track of the daily lowest temperatures in your town over a three-month period in order to look for trends, what would be the best way to display this data?

   A. a pie chart or circle graph

   B. a frequency table

   C. a line graph

   D. a bar graph

Go to next page ➡

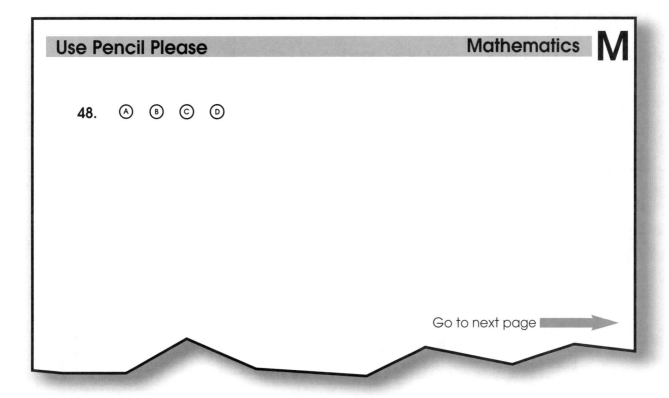

Use Pencil Please

Mathematics **M**

48. Ⓐ Ⓑ Ⓒ Ⓓ

Go to next page ➡

Analysis: *The correct answer is Choice C. Line graphs are best for showing changes over time and they are also good for discovering and comparing trends. In most parts of the United States, if you kept track of the daily lowest temperature, you would be able to spot some sort of a trend, either a gradual warming or a gradual cooling. Choice A is incorrect because pie charts or circle graphs are used to show fractions of a whole. This data is not splitting up some whole thing. Choice B is incorrect because it is not a graphical display. Also, a frequency chart of this data would just be a listing of the number of days where the lowest temperature was 32°, 33°, 34°, and so on. Since temperatures vary widely from one day to the next, the order of the days would get mixed up and it would be much harder to spot a trend. Choice D is incorrect because a bar graph (a horizontal column graph) would show changes going from left to right since the bars are horizontal. We usually think of temperatures as going up and down. However, even a bar graph would be less appropriate than a line graph, because over three months it would have to display over 90 columns. This would be difficult to draw and would make the graph look "busy."*

Question **49** *assesses:*

Data Analysis and Probability Standard

Benchmark F: Determine and use the range, mean, median and mode to analyze and compare data, and explain what each indicates about the data.

4. Understand the different information provided by measures of center (mean, mode and median) and measures of spread (range).

Mathematics **M**

49. Rhonda decided to conduct a survey of all the sixth-graders in her school to find which crayon color each student preferred. The results of her study are summarized in the table below.

Favorite Color	Number of Students
black	16
blue	25
brown	3
green	16
orange	12
red	20
violet	17
yellow	15

Source: www.crayola.com

Which statement is true?

A. The mean of this data is 15.5.

B. The median of this data is lower than its mode.

C. The median of this data is 17.

D. The mean of this data set is higher than its range.

Go to next page ➡

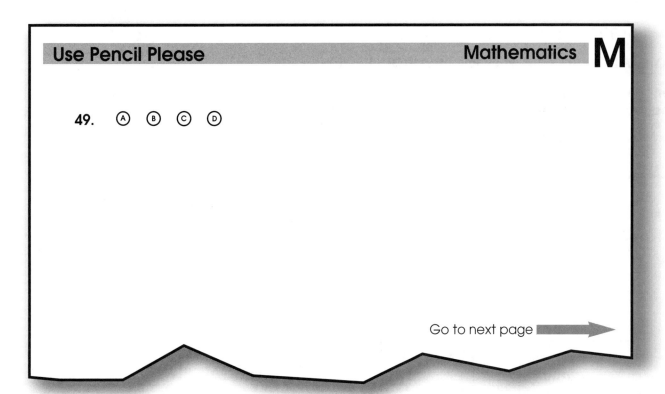

49. (A) (B) (C) (D)

Go to next page ➡

Analysis: *The correct answer is Choice A. To find the mean add up all of the numbers in the data set and divide by eight, the number of numbers in the set: (16 + 25 + 3 + 16 + 12 + 20 + 17 + 15 = 124; 124 ÷ 8 = 15.5). Choice B is incorrect because the median is equal to the mode, not lower. The two middle scores in this data set are both 16. So, the median of the set is 16 (results arranged in increasing order: 3, 12, 15, 16, 16, 17, 20, 25). The most frequent number, the mode, is also 16. Choice C is incorrect because the median of this data set is 16, not 17. Choice D is incorrect because the range of this data set, the difference between the highest and the lowest numbers in the set, is 22 (25 − 3 = 22). Since 22 is greater than the mean which is 15.5, the statement is false.*

Question **50** *assesses:*

Data Analysis and Probability Standard

Benchmark G: Evaluate conjectures and predictions based upon data presented in tables and graphs, and identify misuses of statistical data and displays.

6. Make logical inferences from statistical data.

Mathematics

50. Christine found the following interesting data which relates children's spelling ability to their shoe sizes. A sample of children were given a spelling test. All the scores of children with the same shoe size were averaged together and are presented in the table below.

shoe size	3	4	5	6	7	8
percent of words spelled correctly	15%	25%	33%	47%	64%	83%

Which of the following statements is most likely to be false?

A.   It's hard to know what to make of this data since we don't know how many children were tested and we don't know anything about their ages, grade levels, or even their native languages.

B.   The data clearly shows that the larger a person's shoe size, the better their ability to spell will be.

C.   The increase in spelling ability may be related to the children's ages. The older children tend to have bigger feet than the younger and they also would be in higher grade levels at school. This would tend to make them better spellers.

D.   The experiment should be repeated in another location with different children. Also, many more details of the experiment and the children's backgrounds should be included in the report.

Go to next page ▶

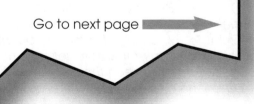

Copying is Prohibited

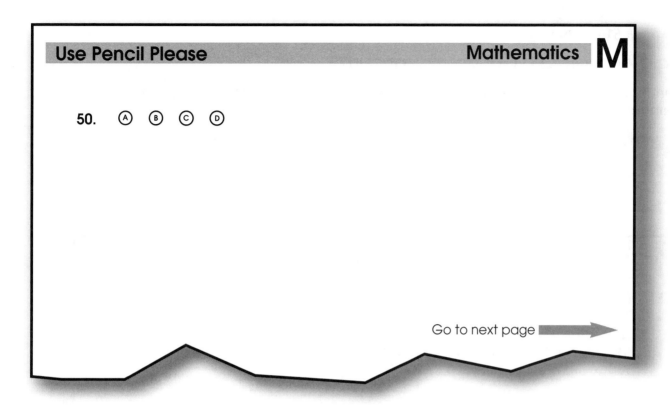

Use Pencil Please   **Mathematics** M

50.   Ⓐ   Ⓑ   Ⓒ   Ⓓ

Go to next page ➤

Analysis: *The correct answer is Choice B since it is the most likely to be false. It seems very unlikely that children with bigger feet would be better spellers if all other factors are equal. Choice A is incorrect because it is true. Next to nothing is stated about the background or number of the children involved in the experiment. This information is vital to judge whether or not conclusions drawn from this data are likely to be valid. Choice C is incorrect because it seems extremely likely to be the real reason for the relationship between shoe size and spelling ability. Of course, this cannot be proven until more is known about the experiment and the children, but is does seem much more likely than the conclusion in Choice B. Choice D is incorrect because it is certainly true. Any scientific experiment must be repeated to show validity.*

Question **51** *assesses:*

Data Analysis and Probability Standard

Benchmark K: Make and justify predictions based on experimental and theoretical probabilities.

7. Design an experiment to test a theoretical probability and explain how the results may vary.

Mathematics

51. Dale and Roy conducted an experiment to test the theoretical probability of flipping a coin. They flipped a quarter 10 times and got 8 heads and 2 tails. As they consider their results, which of the following suggestions will be the least helpful?

   A.   They should continue their experiment, flipping the coin and recording the results several hundred or even a thousand times.

   B.   They should consider adding others to help them with the coin flipping and recording of the results. Maybe several teams could operate at the same time to speed up the data collection process.

   C.   They should remember that theoretical probability may not perfectly predict experimental results. Even very unlikely outcomes do happen, and a high probability is not a guarantee.

   D.   They should consider their experiment a failure since they should have gotten 5 heads and 5 tails.

Go to next page ➡

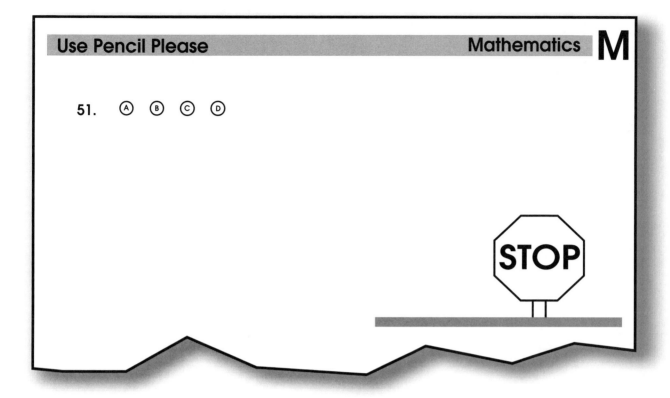

51. Ⓐ Ⓑ Ⓒ Ⓓ

STOP

Analysis: *The correct answer is Choice D because this is the only unhelpful suggestion. Experiments that do not prove your hypothesis are not experiment failures. You certainly need to consider the results and all the factors that contributed to them. Essential considerations include:*

1. Is there something wrong with the design of my experiment?

2. Did I collect enough data?

3. Is there some kind of built-in bias like a dishonest coin?

4. Is there something wrong with my hypothesis?

Mathematicians and scientists try to learn from their mistakes as well as successes. All of the other choices are incorrect, because they are helpful and should be seriously considered.

Mathematics Practice Test 1

Directions:

Today you will be taking a practice Ohio Grade 6 Mathematics Achievement Test. Three different types of questions appear on this test: multiple choice, short answer and extended response.

There are several important things to remember:

1. Read each question carefully. Think about what is being asked. Look carefully at graphs or diagrams because they will help you understand the question.

2. You may use the blank areas of your Student Test Booklet to solve problems. You may also use the optional grid paper in the answer document to solve problems.

3. For short-answer and extended-response questions, use a pencil to write your answers neatly and clearly in the gridded space provided in the answer document. Any answers you write in the Student Test Booklet will not be scored.

4. Short-answer questions are worth two points. Extended-response questions are worth four points. Point values are printed near each question in your Student Test Booklet. The amount of gridded space provided for your answers is the same for all two- and four-point questions.

5. For multiple-choice questions, shade in the circle next to your choice in the answer document for the test question. Mark only one choice for each question. Darken completely the circles on the answer document. If you change an answer, make sure that you erase your old answer completely.

6. Do not spend too much time on one question. Go on to the next question and return to the question skipped after answering the remaining questions.

7. Check over your work when you are finished.

Go to next page

M Mathematics

1. Some students in Mrs. Terran's class were guessing how many inches tall they thought a desk was. Their guesses in inches are shown on the table below.

Name	Guess
Henry	43.81
Gert	$42 \frac{2}{3}$
Drew	43.02
Elliot	$\frac{430}{100}$

After they had guessed, Mrs. Terran told them the desk was 43 inches tall.

Whose guess was the closest to the actual height of the desk?

A. Henry

B. Gert

C. Drew

D. Elliot

2. Milton was watching TV. He was watching channel 10. During a commercial, he flipped 3 channels up. Then, he flipped 5 channels down. Finally, he flipped 7 channels up and 2 channels down.

Which expression can be used to find the channel Milton ended on?

A. $10 + 3 + 5 + 7 + 2$

B. $10 - 3 - 5 + 7 + 2$

C. $10 - 3 + 5 - 7 + 2$

D. $10 + 3 - 5 + 7 - 2$

Go to next page

3. What is the prime factorization of 76?

    A. $2^2 \times 38$

    B. $2^2 \times 19$

    C. 2×38

    D. $2^2 \times 33$

4. What is the greatest common factor of 126 and 154?

    A. 2

    B. 7

    C. 11

    D. 14

5. In the picture below, the amount of water that each measuring cup is holding is shaded.

For question 5, respond completely in your **Answer Document**. (4 points)

In your **Answer Document**, write an expression and find the total amount of water that is held by the three measuring cups.

Go to next page

M Mathematics

6. A parking lot at a shopping mall has 21 rows. The greatest number of cars in any row is 47. The fewest number of cars in any row is 41.

    About how many cars could be in the parking lot?

    A. 700 to 800 cars

    B. 860 to 990 cars

    C. 1,000 to 1,100 cars

    D. 21 to 47 cars

7. For his birthday, Pedro took 63 cookies to share with his class. If there are a total of 21 students in the class, what is the ratio of cookies to students?

    A. 3 to 1

    B. 1 to 3

    C. 7 to 1

    D. 1 to 7

Go to next page

Copying is Prohibited

© Englefield & Associates, Inc.

Mathematics M

8. Rasheed made a model of his tree house. If each inch on the model represents 2 yards, which equation can be used to find P, the perimeter of the actual tree house in yards, using the perimeter of the model, m, in inches?

    A. $P = 2 \times m \div (3 \div 12)$

    B. $P = (2 \times m) \div (12 \div 3)$

    C. $P = 2 \times m$

    D. $P = 2 \times (2 + m)$

9. The table below shows the areas of some rectangles. Each rectangle has a width of 2 units.

Length (Units)	Area (Square Units)
1	2
2	4
3	6
n	

    Which expression can be used to find the area, in square units, of a rectangle with a width of 2 and a length of n units?

    A. $2n^2$

    B. $2n$

    C. $2n + 1$

    D. $2 + n$

Go to next page

M Mathematics

10. Andy is 3 years younger than 2 times his sister's age, *n*.

    In your **Answer Document**, write an equation that can be used to find Andy's age, *a*.

    For question 10, respond completely in your **Answer Document**. (2 points)

11. The zoo had *n* visitors during June. In July, the zoo had 3,019 more visitors than they had in June. In August, they had 427 fewer visitors than in June.

    Which expression could be used to find *v*, the total number of visitors in those 3 months?

    A. $v = n + 3,019 - 427$

    B. $v = n + (n + 3,019) + (n + 3,019 - 427)$

    C. $v = n + (n + 3,019) + (n - 427)$

    D. $v = n + (n + 3,019) - (n - 427)$

Go to next page

12. Which angle below is an obtuse angle?

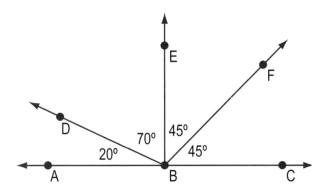

A.   ∠DBF

B.   ∠EBC

C.   ∠DBE

D.   ∠FBC

13. The radius of a tire is about 1 foot. How does the radius compare to the circumference of the tire?

A.   The circumference is about 6 times the radius.

B.   The circumference is about 3 times the radius.

C.   The circumference is about 1 times the radius.

D.   The circumference is not related to the radius.

Go to next page

M Mathematics

14. Sammy was measuring how far a caterpillar moved every hour. During the first hour, the caterpillar moved about 9.4 inches. The caterpillar moved about 11.8 inches during the second hour. In the third hour, the caterpillar moved 13.05 inches.

    Estimate how far the caterpillar moved, in total, during those three hours.

    A.   29 inches

    B.   32 inches

    C.   34 inches

    D.   35 inches

15. Mrs. Oliver's class chose Shannon, Pablo, Mark, and Amy to run a four-mile relay race. Each student ran one mile. Their times are shown in the table below by minutes:seconds.

Name	Time
Shannon	6:27
Pablo	8:31
Mark	6:55
Amy	7:04

What was the total amount of time it took the students from Mrs. Oliver's class to complete the relay race?

    A.   27:57

    B.   28:03

    C.   28:17

    D.   28:57

Go to next page

Mathematics M

16. The sixth graders at Lincoln Elementary School collected cans to recycle. The number of cans each class collected is shown in the table below.

Class	Cans
Mrs. Molyet	225
Mr. Murphy	180
Ms Garn	200
Mrs. Yu	175

Which graph represents the data in the table?

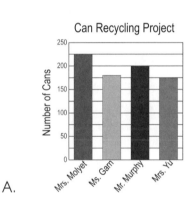

A.

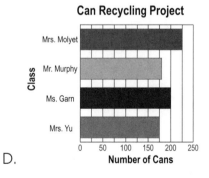

B.

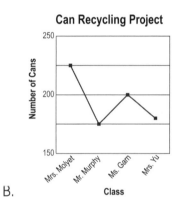

C.

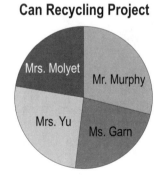

D.

Go to next page

M Mathematics

17. The 5 students from Mrs. Yu's class who collected the most cans in the recycling project are listed in the table below.

Name	Cans
Rachel	27
John	23
Jasmine	17
Ralph	14
Penelope	14

In your **Answer Document**, determine the median of the data. Show work or explain your answer.

For question 17, respond completely in your **Answer Document**. (2 points)

Go to next page

18. Sal, the owner of Sal's Pasta Emporium, took a survey on Friday night to find out what dish people liked the most. The results are shown in the bar graph below.

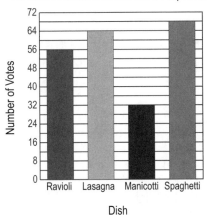

Favorite Dishes at Sal's Pasta Emporium

Which of the following can you learn from the bar graph?

A.   how many people voted for lasagna

B.   the number of people who ate at Sal's Pasta Emporium last week

C.   Sal's favorite dish

D.   how many people like rigatoni best

Go to next page

M Mathematics

19. Eva has a newspaper route. She delivers 13 newspapers every day of the week. On Monday through Saturday, the newspaper cost $0.50 and weighs about 8 ounces. The Sunday newspaper costs $1.50 and weighs twice as much as the regular newspaper.

    In your **Answer Document**, find how many newspapers Eva will deliver in 52 weeks. Show work or explain your answer.

    For question 19, respond completely in your **Answer Document**. (4 points)

20. Angel's mother has 3 children. She had 1 child every 3 years. Angel is 7 years old; it's her birthday. If the oldest child is 1 year younger than twice the youngest child's age, which could be the ages of the children in Angel's family?

    A.   1, 4, 7

    B.   4, 7, 10

    C.   5, 7, 9

    D.   7, 10, 13

Go to next page ➡

Copying is Prohibited
© Englefield & Associates, Inc.

21. The three blocks shown below fit a pattern. A block that does not fit the pattern is also shown. There is a relationship between the shape and the number on each block.

Part of the Pattern   Not Part of the Pattern

Which block belongs in the pattern?

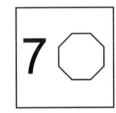

A.

B.

C.

D.

Go to next page

M Mathematics

22. Albert thought that if a triangle and a square had the same height, the area of the square would always be bigger. Is Albert correct?

    A.   Yes; you need to divide to find the area of a triangle, but you do not have to use division to find the area of a square.

    B.   Yes; squares have a greater number of sides than triangles.

    C.   No; without knowing the length of the triangle's base, you cannot compare the shapes.

    D.   No; triangles always have larger areas than squares.

23. Look at the number line below.

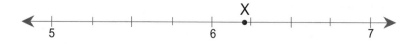

    Which of the following is closest to point X?

    A.   6.02

    B. $5\frac{4}{5}$

    C. $\frac{19}{3}$

    D.   6.20

Go to next page

24. Ronaldo was given the following problem to solve.

    $$52 - 4(5 + 7) \div 6$$

    Which choice lists the correct order of operations Ronaldo must use to solve the problem?

    A.   multiplication, division, subtraction, addition

    B.   multiplication, addition, subtraction, division

    C.   addition, multiplication, division, subtraction

    D.   addition, multiplication, subtraction, division

25. Which equation can be used to find the number of days, d, in y years?

    A. $d = y \times 12$

    B. $d = y + 365$

    C. $d = y \div 365$

    D. $d = y \times 365$

Go to next page

M Mathematics

26. Rose is 12 years old. Grace is older than Rose. What is the relationship between Rose's age (r) and Grace's age (g)?

    A. $r > g$

    B. $r \geq g$

    C. $r \leq g$

    D. $r < g$

27. A plate has a diameter of 9 inches. How does the size of the radius of the plate compare to the size of the diameter of the plate?

    A. The radius is half the size of the diameter.

    B. The radius is two times the size of the diameter.

    C. The radius is about three times the size of the diameter.

    D. The radius is about four and a half times the size of the diameter.

Go to next page

Copying is Prohibited

© Englefield & Associates, Inc.

28. A candy company makes boxes of chocolates. Each box contains 14 chocolates with nuts and 18 chocolates without nuts. The company can make 608 chocolates per hour.

   In your **Answer Document**, determine how many of the 608 chocolates will have nuts. Show work or explain your answer.

For question 28, respond completely in your **Answer Document**. (2 points)

Go to next page

M Mathematics

29. Each sixth-grade student can compete in 1 of 4 events on field day. Each student chooses which event he or she wants to compete in. The choices are shown in the graph below. On field day, however, the relay race has to be cancelled, and the students who signed up for the relay race must choose a new event to compete in.

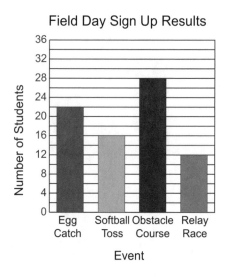

After each student signs up for a new event, what is the greatest number of students that could compete in any 1 event?

A. 28 students

B. 34 students

C. 36 students

D. 40 students

Go to next page ▬▬▬▶

© Englefield & Associates, Inc.

Mathematics M

30. Look at the diagram below.

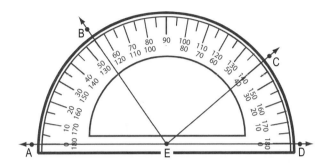

In your **Answer Document**, determine the measure of ∠BEC to the nearest degree.

For question 30, respond completely in your **Answer Document**. (2 points)

31. Look at the number sequence below.

1, 1, 2, 3, 5, 8, 13, 21, 34

What are the next two numbers in the sequence below?

In your **Answer Document**, explain how you arrived at your answer.

For question 31, respond completely in your **Answer Document**. (4 points)

Go to next page ▶

M   Mathematics

32. Look at the drawings below.

All of these expressions represent the shaded region except

A. $\frac{2}{16}$

B. $3\frac{1}{2}$

C. $\frac{7}{2}$

D.   3.5

Go to next page ▶

33. Allison threw 2 darts at the board shown below.

1 point	3 points
4 points	2 points

If both darts landed somewhere on the board, what is the probability that she scored less than 4 points total?

A. $\frac{3}{16}$

B. $\frac{1}{3}$

C. $\frac{3}{8}$

D. $\frac{3}{4}$

Go to next page

M | Mathematics

34. Look at the drawing below.

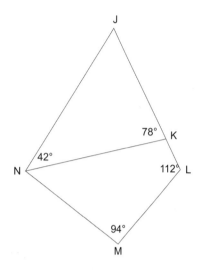

What is the measure of ∠KNM?

A.   52°

B.   60°

C.   94°

D.   102°

35. Each morning, Elijah takes a handful of coins from the table to buy lunch. When he comes home each afternoon, he puts back what he hasn't used. On Monday, there were 19 coins on the table. He took 5 coins in the morning and put 1 back in the afternoon. On Tuesday, Elijah only needed 4 coins in the morning; he put 2 back that afternoon. Wednesday was pizza day, so Elijah took 7 coins with him and brought home 1 coin in the afternoon.

Which expression can be used to find how many coins are on the table at the end of the day on Tuesday?

A. $5 + 1 - 4 + 2 - 7 + 1$

B. $19 - 5 + 1 - 4 + 2 - 7 + 1$

C. $19 - 5 + 1 - 4 + 2$

D. $19 + 5 - 1 + 4 - 2 + 7 - 1$

36. Kyle is helping to fix playground equipment at a local park. He is responsible for increasing the size of the sandbox, which is 4 feet by 6 feet. To do this, he will add 2 feet to the width of the sandbox.

In your **Answer Document**, determine the new perimeter of the sandbox after Kyle adds 2 feet to the width. Show work or explain your answer.

For question 36, respond completely in your **Answer Document**. (4 points)

Go to next page

M Mathematics

37. Skip wants to add a row of carrots and a row of corn to his garden this year. He also wants to install a 4-foot high chain link fence around the garden to keep the rabbits from eating his produce.

What does Skip need to know in order to determine how much of the fencing he will need to protect his crops?

   A.　the surface area of the garden

   B.　the area of the garden

   C.　the perimeter of the garden

   D.　the area of the fence

38. The graph below shows the number of goals Lucy scored in each of the first 7 soccer games this season.

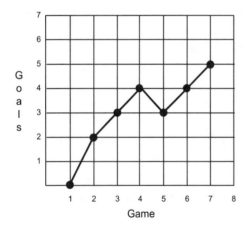

What is the mean of Lucy's goals scored for the first 7 games?

   A.　1

   B.　2

   C.　3

   D.　4

Go to next page

　　　　Copying is Prohibited　　　　© Englefield & Associates, Inc.

Mathematics M

39. Keenan wants to fill the flower box below with soil.

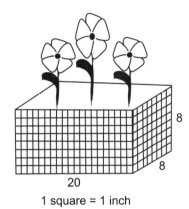

8

8

20

1 square = 1 inch

About how much soil will Keenan need to fill the box to the top with soil?

A.   1280 cubic inches

B.   640 cubic inches

C.   512 cubic inches

D.   160 cubic inches

Go to next page

M **Mathematics**

40. Rufus wants to paint the bike ramp below. One can of paint will cover 15 square feet.

What information does Rufus need to figure out to know whether he has enough paint to cover the ramp?

A.   the volume of the ramp

B.   the perimeter of the ramp

C.   the surface area of the ramp

D.   the radius of the ramp

Optional Grid Paper

NOTHING ON THIS PAGE WILL BE SCORED

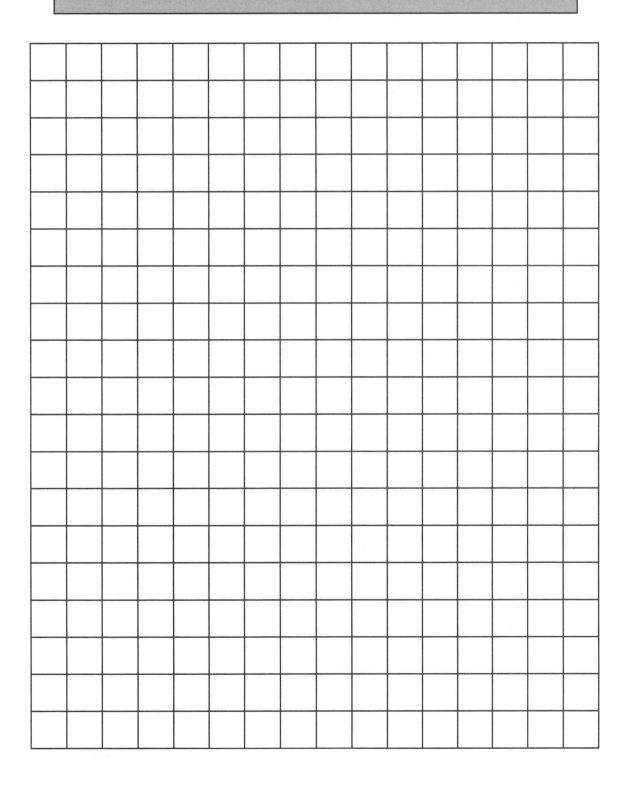

M Mathematics

Use Pencil Please

1. Ⓐ Ⓑ Ⓒ Ⓓ

2. Ⓐ Ⓑ Ⓒ Ⓓ

3. Ⓐ Ⓑ Ⓒ Ⓓ

4. Ⓐ Ⓑ Ⓒ Ⓓ

5. Write your response to question 5 in the space below.

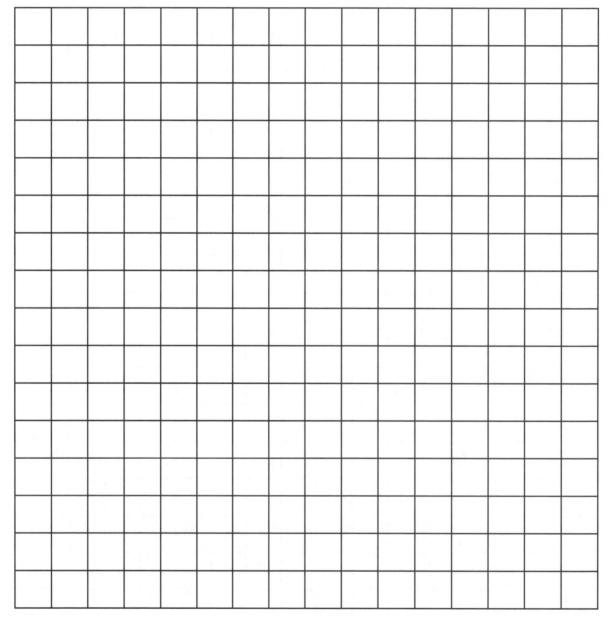

Go to next page ➡

Copying is Prohibited © Englefield & Associates, Inc.

Mathematics M

6. Ⓐ Ⓑ Ⓒ Ⓓ

7. Ⓐ Ⓑ Ⓒ Ⓓ

8. Ⓐ Ⓑ Ⓒ Ⓓ

9. Ⓐ Ⓑ Ⓒ Ⓓ

10. Write your response to question 10 in the space below.

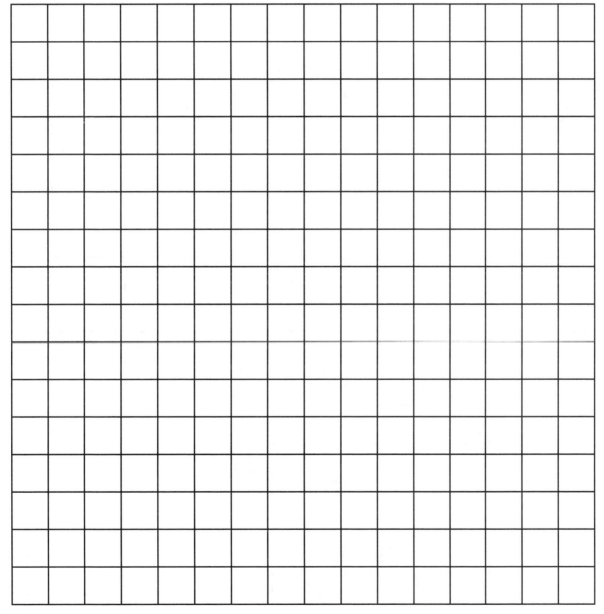

11. Ⓐ Ⓑ Ⓒ Ⓓ

Go to next page ▶

M Mathematics   Use Pencil Please

12. Ⓐ Ⓑ Ⓒ Ⓓ

13. Ⓐ Ⓑ Ⓒ Ⓓ

14. Ⓐ Ⓑ Ⓒ Ⓓ

15. Ⓐ Ⓑ Ⓒ Ⓓ

16. Ⓐ Ⓑ Ⓒ Ⓓ

17. Write your response to question 17 in the space below.

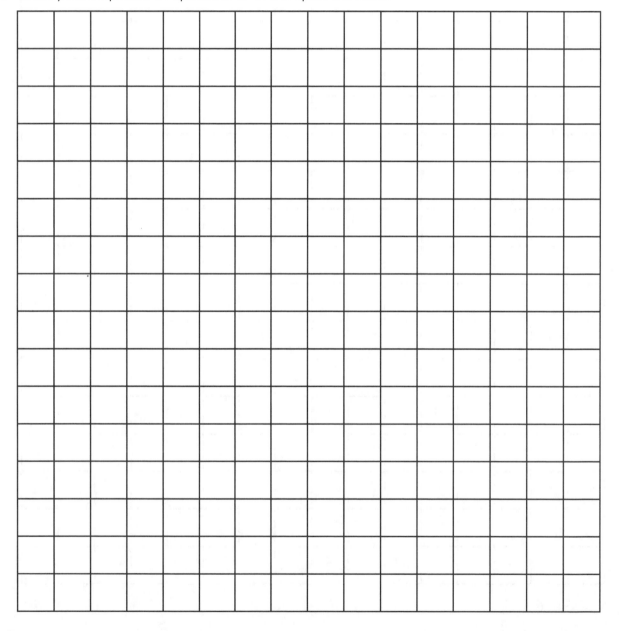

Go to next page ▶

Copying is Prohibited
© Englefield & Associates, Inc.

Mathematics **M**

18. Ⓐ   Ⓑ   Ⓒ   Ⓓ

19. Write your response to question 19 in the space below.

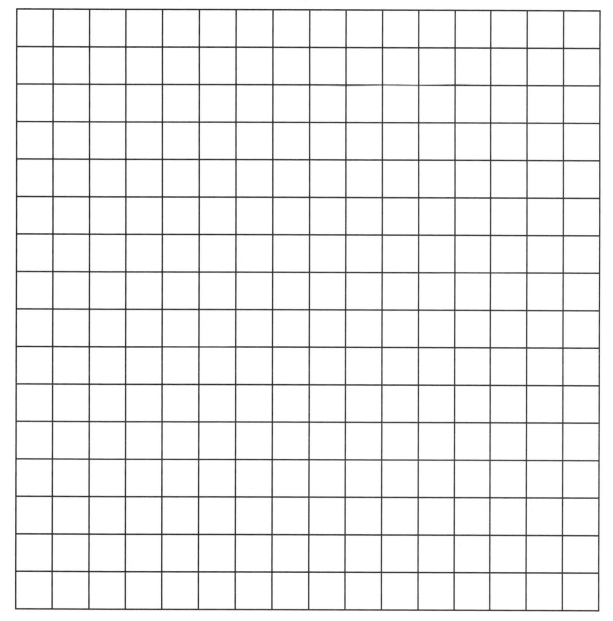

20. Ⓐ   Ⓑ   Ⓒ   Ⓓ

21. Ⓐ   Ⓑ   Ⓒ   Ⓓ

22. Ⓐ   Ⓑ   Ⓒ   Ⓓ

23. Ⓐ   Ⓑ   Ⓒ   Ⓓ

Go to next page

M Mathematics   Use Pencil Please

24. Ⓐ Ⓑ Ⓒ Ⓓ

25. Ⓐ Ⓑ Ⓒ Ⓓ

26. Ⓐ Ⓑ Ⓒ Ⓓ

27. Ⓐ Ⓑ Ⓒ Ⓓ

28. Write your response to question 28 in the space below.

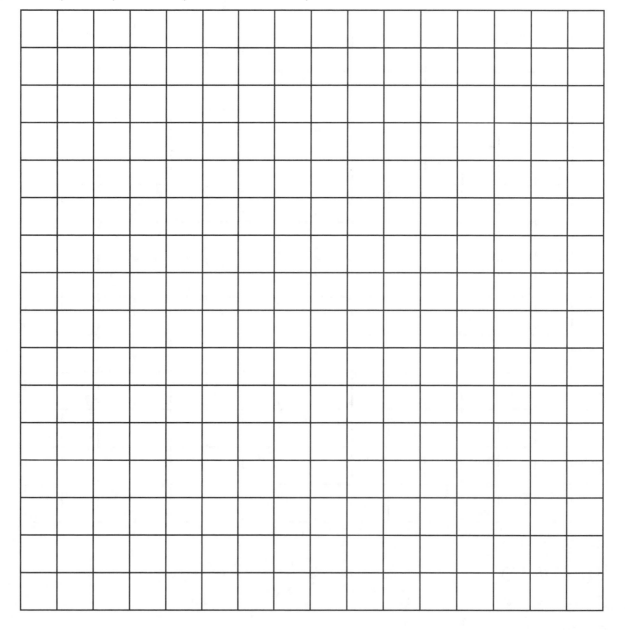

Go to next page ➤

Copying is Prohibited

Mathematics M

29. Ⓐ Ⓑ Ⓒ Ⓓ

30. Write your response to question 30 in the space below.

Go to next page

M Mathematics

Use Pencil Please

31. Write your response to question 31 in the space below.

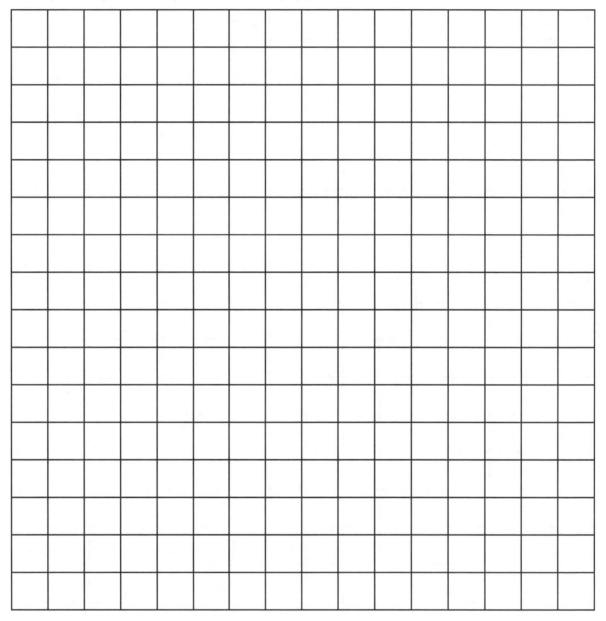

32. Ⓐ　Ⓑ　Ⓒ　Ⓓ

33. Ⓐ　Ⓑ　Ⓒ　Ⓓ

34. Ⓐ　Ⓑ　Ⓒ　Ⓓ

35. Ⓐ　Ⓑ　Ⓒ　Ⓓ

Go to next page ➡

Copying is Prohibited
© Englefield & Associates, Inc.

36. Write your response to question 36 in the space below.

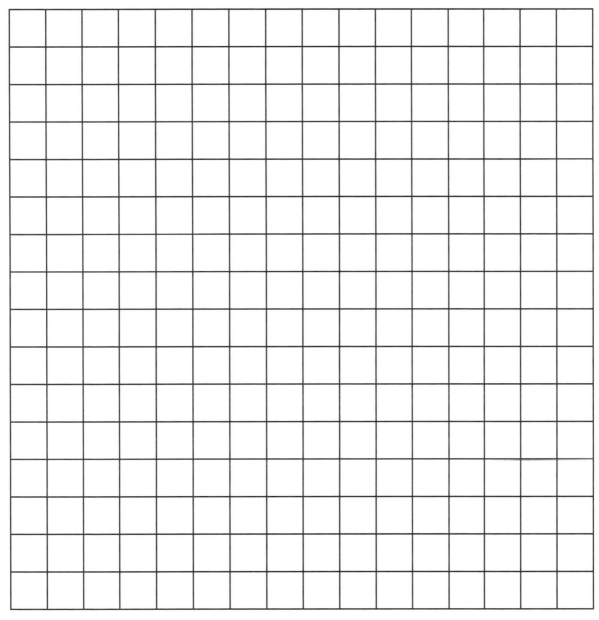

37. Ⓐ   Ⓑ   Ⓒ   Ⓓ

38. Ⓐ   Ⓑ   Ⓒ   Ⓓ

39. Ⓐ   Ⓑ   Ⓒ   Ⓓ

40. Ⓐ   Ⓑ   Ⓒ   Ⓓ

Mathematics Practice Test 2

Directions:

Today you will be taking a practice Ohio Grade 6 Mathematics Achievement Test. Three different types of questions appear on this test: multiple choice, short answer and extended response.

There are several important things to remember:

1. Read each question carefully. Think about what is being asked. Look carefully at graphs or diagrams because they will help you understand the question.

2. You may use the blank areas of your Student Test Booklet to solve problems. You may also use the optional grid paper in the answer document to solve problems.

3. For short-answer and extended-response questions, use a pencil to write your answers neatly and clearly in the gridded space provided in the answer document. Any answers you write in the Student Test Booklet will not be scored.

4. Short-answer questions are worth two points. Extended-response questions are worth four points. Point values are printed near each question in your Student Test Booklet. The amount of gridded space provided for your answers is the same for all two- and four-point questions.

5. For multiple-choice questions, shade in the circle next to your choice in the answer document for the test question. Mark only one choice for each question. Darken completely the circles on the answer document. If you change an answer, make sure that you erase your old answer completely.

6. Do not spend too much time on one question. Go on to the next question and return to the question skipped after answering the remaining questions.

7. Check over your work when you are finished.

Go to next page ▶

M Mathematics

1. Duncan and Debby each had 6 cookies. Of Duncan's cookies, 2 were chocolate chip. Debby had 4 chocolate chip cookies. Which fraction shows how many of the cookies were chocolate chip?

    A. $\frac{1}{6}$

    B. $\frac{1}{3}$

    C. $\frac{1}{2}$

    D. $\frac{2}{3}$

2. Rosa's math test scores are 9.3, 8.8, 7.3, and 9.9.

    In your **Answer Document** find the sum of her test scores.

    For question 2, respond completely in your **Answer Document**. (2 points)

3. A 250-piece puzzle has 70 border pieces. What is the ratio of border pieces to the total number of pieces in the puzzle?

    A. $\frac{7}{25}$

    B. $\frac{7}{18}$

    C. $\frac{18}{25}$

    D. $\frac{1}{7}$

Go to next page

Mathematics M

4.   Look at the conversion chart below.

> 8 ounces = 1 cup
> 2 cups = 1 pint

Which equation can be used to find the number of ounces, *o*, in *p*, pints?

A. $o = p \times (8 \div 2)$

B. $o = p \times (8 \times 2)$

C. $o = p \div (8 \times 2)$

D. $o = p \times (8 - 2)$

5.   The table below shows the area of some triangles with various heights.

Height (Units)	Area (Square Units)
1	2.5
2	5
3	7.5

Which expression can be used to find the area, in square units, of a triangle with a height of 5 and a base of *n* units?

A. $n + 2.5$

B. $(n \times 2) \div 5$

C. $(2 \times 5) \div n$

D. $(n \times 5) \div 2$

Go to next page

M Mathematics

6. Dan threw a discus *n* feet. Carl threw a discus twice as far as Dan. Sergei threw a discus 5 feet less than Carl.

    Which equation can be used to find *T*, the total number of feet they threw?

    A. $T = n + 2n - 5$

    B. $T = n + 2n + (n - 5)$

    C. $T = n + 2n + (2n - 5)$

    D. $T = n + 2(2n - 5)$

7. Look at the quadrilateral below.

    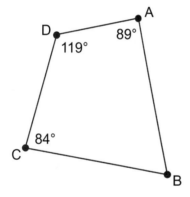

    In your **Answer Document**, determine the measure of ∠ABC in degrees. Show work or explain your answer.

    For question 7, respond completely in your **Answer Document**. (2 points)

Go to next page ➡

8. Three Bavaro children collect coins. The children gave up their individual collections to make one large collection. The amounts contributed by the children are shown in the circle graph. When Mr. Bavaro looked at the graph, he realized the children did not label each section.

Coins of the Bavaro Children

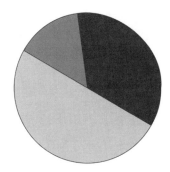

Which table contains the data the circle graph represents?

A.

Name	Coins
Phil	8
Lisa	12
Carmen	4

B.

Name	Coins
Phil	12
Lisa	6
Carmen	10

C.

Name	Coins
Phil	11
Lisa	10
Carmen	12

D.

Name	Coins
Phil	16
Lisa	5
Carmen	7

Go to next page

M Mathematics

9. Yoshi was given the following problem to solve.

$$5 + 4 \times (8 \div 2) - 1$$

He wrote down the following plan to solve the problem.

1. Divide 8 by 2: $5 + 4 \times (4) - 1$
2. Add 5 and 4: $9 \times (4) - 1$
3. Multiply 9 and 4: $36 - 1$
4. Subtract 1 from 36: 35

Did Yoshi make a mistake? If so, what was his mistake?

A.   Yes, he should have performed all multiplication before adding.

B.   Yes, he should have performed all subtraction before multiplying.

C.   Yes, he should have performed all addition before dividing.

D.   No, he solved the problem correctly.

Go to next page

10. Hiram and Jethro were having a fishing contest. Whoever caught the most fish was the winner. Hiram caught f number of fish in the first hour, and Jethro caught 4 more fish than Hiram caught. In the second hour, Hiram caught 4 more fish than the number of fish Jethro caught. In the third hour, Jethro's total exceeded the number of fish caught by Hiram by 4. In the fourth and final hour, Hiram and Jethro each caught 8 fish.

   Which of the following is true?

   A.   Hiram won the contest.

   B.   Jethro won the contest.

   C.   They tied.

   D.   There is no way to tell who won.

11. Mrs. Detoto gave her class the following group of numbers that share a common characteristic.

   8, 15, 24, 48

   Which of the numbers below shares a common characteristic with the numbers above and why?

   A.   The number 23, because it is a prime number.

   B.   The number 32, because it is a multiple of 8.

   C.   The number 44, because it is an even number.

   D.   The number 80, because it is 1 less than a perfect square.

Go to next page

M Mathematics

12. The table below shows the number of lawns Adam mows each day of the week.

Day	Sunday	Monday	Tuesday	Wednesday	Thursday	Friday	Saturday
Lawns	6	1	2	3	1	1	4

What is the range of the data?

A. 1

B. 2

C. 5

D. 6

Go to next page ➤

© Englefield & Associates, Inc.

13. The figures shown below are both rectangles.

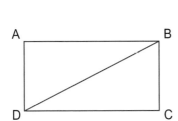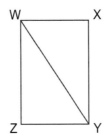

Which angle pairs must be congruent?

A.   ∠WYZ and ∠WYX

B.   ∠ZWY and ∠CDB

C.   ∠BDA and ∠ZYW

D.   ∠DAB and ∠WXY

14. Ernie ate one-fourth of the cookies in the cookie jar.
Julio ate one-third of the cookies in the cookie jar. Liv
ate one-twelfth of the cookies in the cookie jar.

What fraction of the cookies were left in the cookie jar
after Ernie, Julio, and Liv ate their cookies?

A. $\frac{1}{4}$

B. $\frac{1}{3}$

C. $\frac{2}{3}$

D. $\frac{3}{4}$

Go to next page

M Mathematics

15. The top of Frida's drum has a diameter of 11 inches.

    Which formula can Frida use to find the circumference of the top of her drum?

    A. $\pi \times 11$

    B. $\pi \times 5.5$

    C. $\pi \times 11^2$

    D. $\pi \times 5.5^2$

16. Maria has an amount of money, *n*, saved in the bank. In her piggybank at home, she has $2.00 less than half of the amount she has in the bank.

    In your **Answer Document**, write an equation that can be used to find m, the total amount of money Maria has saved.

    For question 16, respond completely in your **Answer Document**. (2 points)

17. Mr. Jimenez gave his class a group of numbers that share a common characteristic.

    2, 5, 11

    He then told them 7 could also be included with the group, but 10 could not. Why does the number 7 belong with this group of numbers?

    A.   It is an odd number.

    B.   It is a perfect square.

    C.   It is a prime factor of 770.

    D.   It is a multiple of 440.

Go to next page

Mathematics M

18. In your **Answer Document**, determine the least common multiple of 16 and 36. Show work or explain your answer.

For question 18, respond completely in your **Answer Document**. (4 points)

19. A grocery store assembles 45 fruit baskets. In the fruit baskets, there are a total of 225 bananas, 180 oranges, 135 apples, and 45 pineapples. What is the ratio of apples to oranges?

    A. 3 to 1

    B. 4 to 1

    C. 3 to 4

    D. 4 to 3

20. During one week in the town of Neva, it snowed every day. The most it snowed on any of those days was 8.4 inches. The least it snowed on any of those days was 4.9 inches. Which is the best estimate of the least amount of snow Neva might have received that week?

    A. 35 inches

    B. 38 inches

    C. 43 inches

    D. 53 inches

Go to next page

M Mathematics

21. The diameters and areas of some circles are given in the table below.

Diameter (Units)	Area (Square Units)
2	π
4	4π
6	9π
8	16π
n	

Which expression can be used to find the area, in square units, of a circle with a diameter of n units?

A. $\left(\dfrac{n}{2}\right)^2 \times \pi$

B. $\dfrac{n^2}{2} \times \pi$

C. $\dfrac{n^2 \times \pi}{2}$

D. $n^2 \times \pi$

Go to next page ➤

22. Look at the figure below.

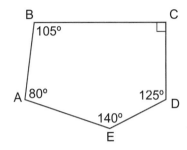

What type of angle is ∠B?

A. acute

B. obtuse

C. right

D. supplemental

Go to next page

M Mathematics

23. Samantha is going to the grocery store for her mother. The list of things her mother gave her to buy is as follows: 5 apples, 1 loaf of bread, 2 gallons of milk, and $\frac{1}{2}$ pound of salami. When she gets to the store, she sees the following signs.

Bread	1 Gallon of Milk	Apples
$1.29	**98¢**	**30¢** each
per loaf		

Salami
$4.16
per pound

In your **Answer Document**, determine how much money, in dollars, Samantha will spend. Show work or explain your answer.

For question 23, respond completely in your **Answer Document**. (4 points)

24. A box of crayons contains 64 crayons. Which equation can be used to find the number of crayons, c, in b boxes of crayons?

 A. $b = c \times 64$

 B. $b = c + 64$

 C. $c = b \times 64$

 D. $c = b + 64$

Go to next page ➡

25. Charles was doing an experiment in his science class. With the help of his teacher, he heated a liquid until it reached 330° F. After he stopped heating the liquid, he recorded its temperature every 2 minutes. He noticed the data formed a pattern. Some of his data is shown in the table below.

Time	Temperature
4 minutes	286°F
8 minutes	242°F
12 minutes	198°F
16 minutes	154°F
20 minutes	110°F

Based on his results, how many seconds after he stopped heating the liquid was its temperature 176°F?

A. 154 seconds

B. 720 seconds

C. 760 seconds

D. 840 seconds

26. Jess has 3 pieces of string. The lengths of the strings are 13 inches, 5 feet, and 2 yards. Look at the problem-solving steps shown below.

Step A: Find the sum of the lengths of string in inches.

Step B: Convert from feet to inches.

Step C: Convert from yards to feet.

In your **Answer Document**, order the steps correctly and find the total length of string in inches. Show work or explain your answer.

For question 26, respond completely in your **Answer Document**. (4 points)

 Go to next page

M Mathematics

27. A large box of nails holds n nails. A small box of nails holds 100 fewer nails than the large box. If the company that produces the nails adds 50 nails to each large box to make an extra-large box, which equation can be used to find T, the total number of nails in an extra-large box and a small box?

   A. $T = (n + 50) + (n - 50)$

   B. $T = (n + 50) - (n - 50)$

   C. $T = (n) + (n - 50)$

   D. $T = (n + 50) + (n - 100)$

28. Leah wants to create a rotation of figure RSTU. So far, she has drawn WXY.

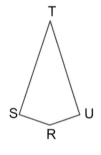

   Which point should she use to complete WXY so that it is a rotation of RSTU?

   A. Point A

   B. Point B

   C. Point C

   D. Point D

Go to next page

29. In which diagram is the unshaded figure a reflection of the shaded figure?

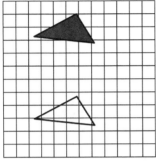

A.

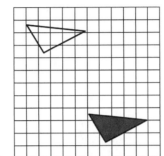

B.

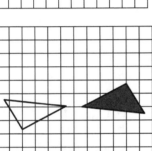

C.

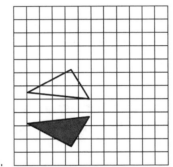

D.

30. Which shape has both parallel sides and perpendicular sides?

A. circle

B. triangle

C. sphere

D. rectangle

Go to next page

M | **Mathematics**

31. Look at the drawing below.

one square = one inch

In your **Answer Document**, determine the perimeter of the business card shown above. Show work or explain your answer.

For question 31, respond completely in your **Answer Document**. (2 points)

Go to next page

Mathematics M

32. Look at the line graph below.

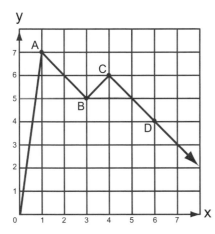

Which table represents the coordinates of the points on the line graph?

A.

Point	x	y
A	1	7
B	3	5
C	4	6
D	6	4

B.

Point	x	y
A	7	1
B	5	3
C	6	4
D	4	6

C.

Point	x	y
A	1	7
B	3	5
C	4	6
D	6	3

D.

Point	x	y
A	7	1
B	5	3
C	6	4
D	3	6

M Mathematics

33. Trevor was given the following figures and was told they have something in common.

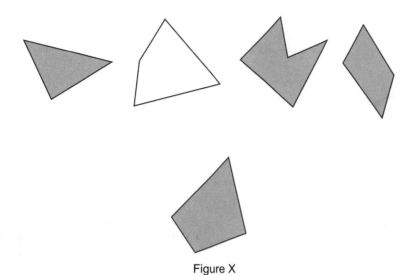

Figure X

Which of the following statements explains why Figure X belongs with the other figures?

A.   It is shaded.

B.   It has an even number of sides.

C.   It has fewer than 6 sides.

D.   It is not a triangle.

Go to next page

34. Which of the following measures would be the most appropriate for describing the difference in height between the tallest and shortest students in a middle school class?

   A.   mean

   B.   median

   C.   mode

   D.   range

Go to next page

M Mathematics

35. The 1993 revenue for the Pitzulo Spaghetti Sauce Company is shown on the graph below.

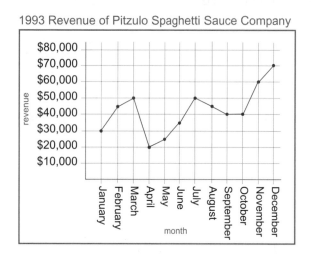

1993 Revenue of Pitzulo Spaghetti Sauce Company

In your **Answer Document**, determine the value of the greatest increase in revenue in dollars from one month to the next. Show work or explain your answer.

For question 35, respond completely in your **Answer Document**. (2 points)

36. The students in Mr. Studer's class made a welcome banner. The radius of the banner was 5 feet. It had purple letters. On the banner, there was also a triangle inside of a square. What shape is the banner?

   A. triangle

   B. square

   C. circle

   D. rectangle

Go to next page ➡

© Englefield & Associates, Inc.

37. Freddy, Gina, and Oscar are putting together a puzzle. So far, Freddy has put together five-sixteenths of the puzzle, Gina has put together one-fourth of the puzzle, and Oscar has put together three-eighths of the puzzle. Which expression can be used to find out how much of the puzzle is not put together?

A. $\frac{16}{16} - \left(\frac{5}{16} + \frac{4}{16} + \frac{6}{16} \right)$

B. $\frac{16}{16} - \frac{5}{16} + \frac{4}{16} + \frac{6}{16}$

C. $\frac{16}{16} - \left(\frac{5}{16} - \frac{4}{16} - \frac{6}{16} \right)$

D. $\frac{5}{16} + \frac{4}{16} + \frac{6}{16}$

38. What is the prime factorization of 56?

A. $2 \times 3 \times 7$

B. $2^2 \times 3 \times 7$

C. $2^3 \times 7$

D. $3^2 \times 5 + 11$

Go to next page

M | Mathematics

39. A floor tile has 52 spots on it. Which proportion could not be used to find the number of spots, *s*, that would be expected to be on 89 tiles?

    A. $\frac{1}{89} = \frac{s}{52}$

    B. $\frac{s}{89} = \frac{52}{1}$

    C. $\frac{89}{s} = \frac{1}{52}$

    D. $\frac{52}{s} = \frac{1}{89}$

40. Kevin's dad wants to widen their driveway so that it can be used as a basketball court. The driveway is 8 feet wide by 25 feet long. The original area is 200 square feet. What will the area of the driveway be if they add 10 feet to the width of the driveway?

    A.   500 square feet

    B.   450 square feet

    C.   400 square feet

    D.   375 square feet

Optional Grid Paper

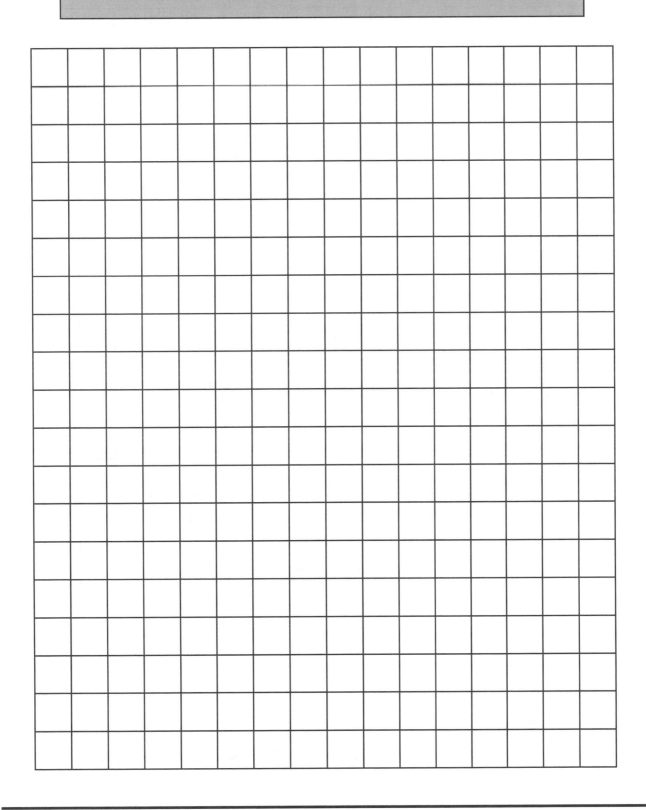

M Mathematics

Use Pencil Please

1. Ⓐ Ⓑ Ⓒ Ⓓ

2. Write your response to question 2 in the space below.

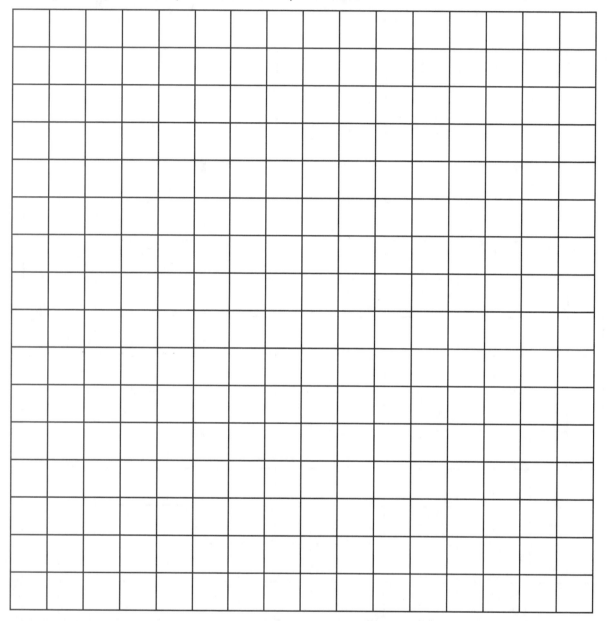

3. Ⓐ Ⓑ Ⓒ Ⓓ

4. Ⓐ Ⓑ Ⓒ Ⓓ

5. Ⓐ Ⓑ Ⓒ Ⓓ

6. Ⓐ Ⓑ Ⓒ Ⓓ

Go to next page ➡

Mathematics M

7. Write your response to question 7 in the space below.

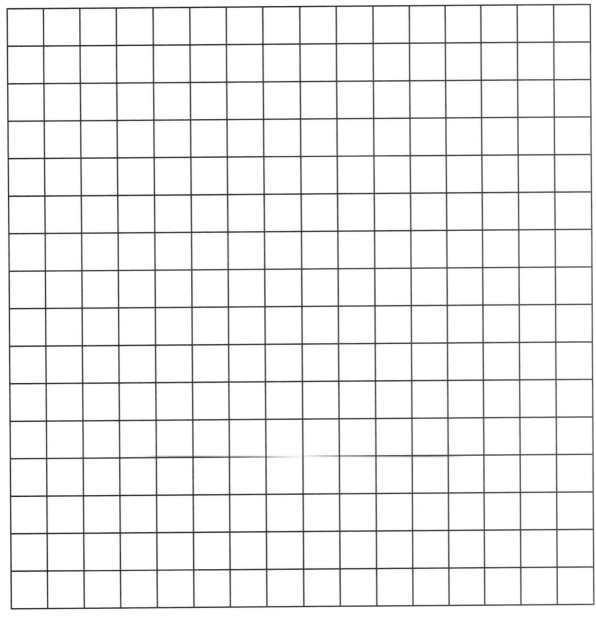

8. Ⓐ Ⓑ Ⓒ Ⓓ

9. Ⓐ Ⓑ Ⓒ Ⓓ

10. Ⓐ Ⓑ Ⓒ Ⓓ

11. Ⓐ Ⓑ Ⓒ Ⓓ

12. Ⓐ Ⓑ Ⓒ Ⓓ

Go to next page ➤

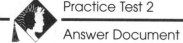
M Mathematics   **Use Pencil Please**

13. Ⓐ Ⓑ Ⓒ Ⓓ

14. Ⓐ Ⓑ Ⓒ Ⓓ

15. Ⓐ Ⓑ Ⓒ Ⓓ

16. Write your response to question 16 in the space below.

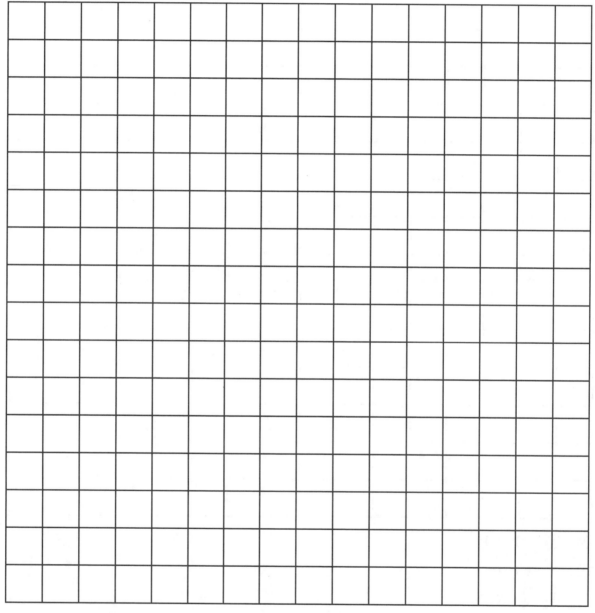

17. Ⓐ Ⓑ Ⓒ Ⓓ

Go to next page ▶

Mathematics M

18. Write your response to question 18 in the space below.

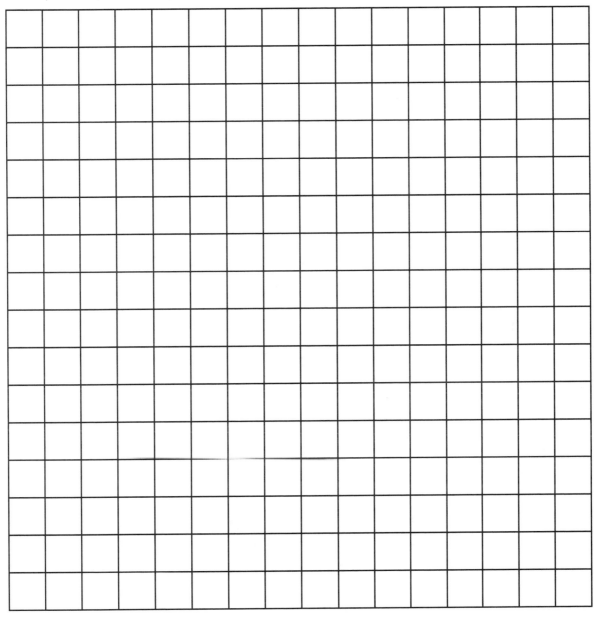

19. Ⓐ Ⓑ Ⓒ Ⓓ

20. Ⓐ Ⓑ Ⓒ Ⓓ

21. Ⓐ Ⓑ Ⓒ Ⓓ

22. Ⓐ Ⓑ Ⓒ Ⓓ

Go to next page

M Mathematics

Use Pencil Please

23. Write your response to question 23 in the space below.

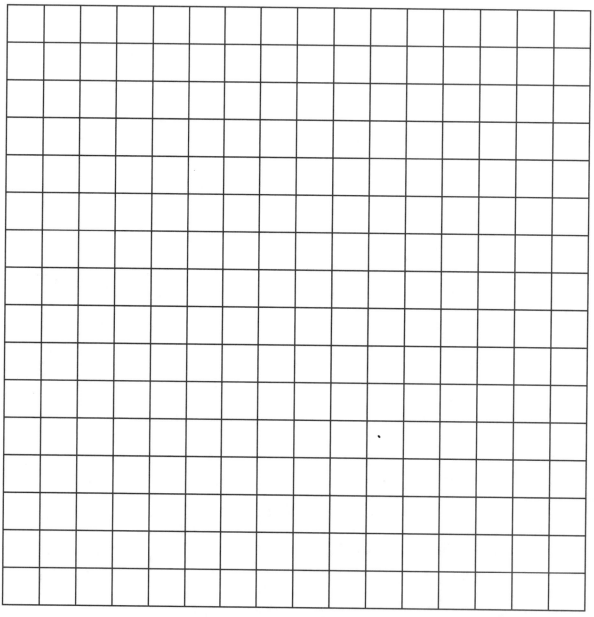

24. Ⓐ Ⓑ Ⓒ Ⓓ

25. Ⓐ Ⓑ Ⓒ Ⓓ

Go to next page ▶

26. Write your response to question 26 in the space below.

27. Ⓐ Ⓑ Ⓒ Ⓓ

28. Ⓐ Ⓑ Ⓒ Ⓓ

29. Ⓐ Ⓑ Ⓒ Ⓓ

30. Ⓐ Ⓑ Ⓒ Ⓓ

Go to next page

M Mathematics

31. Write your response to question 31 in the space below.

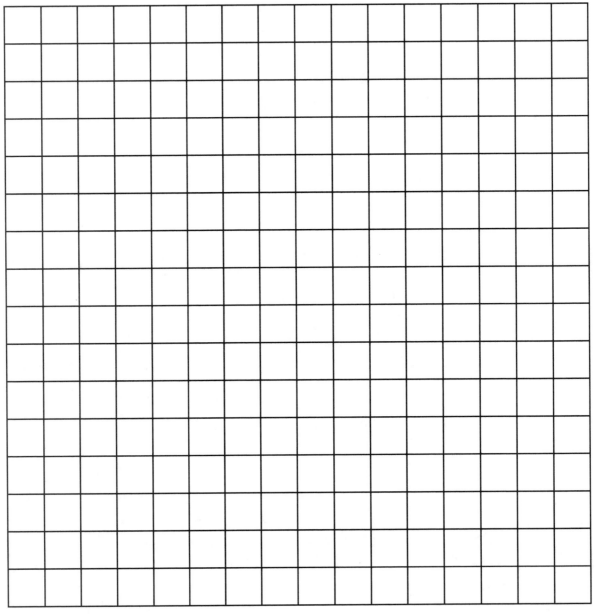

32. Ⓐ Ⓑ Ⓒ Ⓓ

33. Ⓐ Ⓑ Ⓒ Ⓓ

34. Ⓐ Ⓑ Ⓒ Ⓓ

Go to next page ▶

35. Write your response to question 35 in the space below.

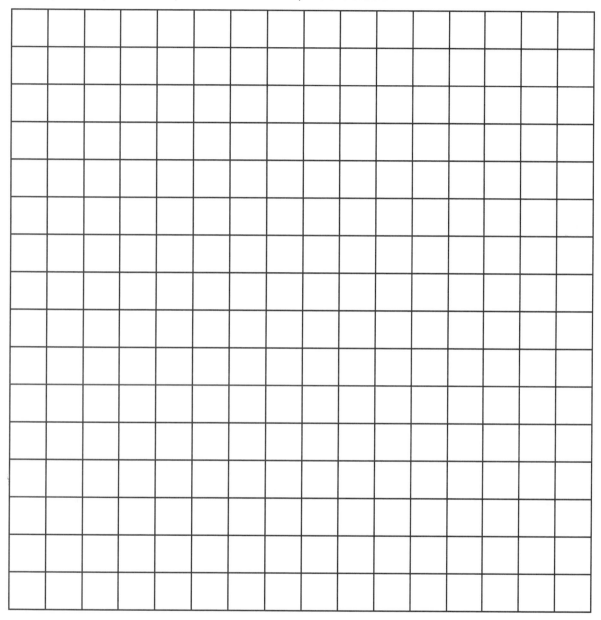

36. Ⓐ Ⓑ Ⓒ Ⓓ

37. Ⓐ Ⓑ Ⓒ Ⓓ

38. Ⓐ Ⓑ Ⓒ Ⓓ

39. Ⓐ Ⓑ Ⓒ Ⓓ

40. Ⓐ Ⓑ Ⓒ Ⓓ

Notes

Notes

Notes

Notes

Show What You Know® on the OAT for Grade 6, Additional Products

Student Workbook and Parent/Teacher Supplement for Reading

Flash Cards for Mathematics and Reading

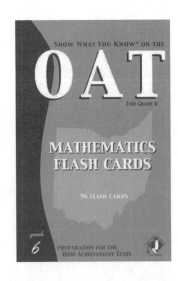

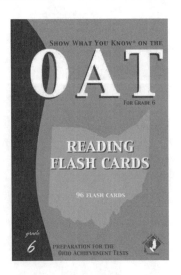